Praise for
Braving the Workplace

"It's no wonder that Beth is the world's leading expert on belonging. She is a true leader, and *Braving the Workplace* will change your life. The world needs Beth's message and she will transform the way you show up in your own life. Everyone needs to read this book, *everyone!*"

—Chester Elton, #1 *New York Times* bestselling author of *All In and Leading with Gratitude*

"*Braving the Workplace* addresses one of the least talked-about dynamics of the workplace. What does it mean to belong at work? Through Beth's personal experience and careful research, she has given us a guide to doing more than just fitting in at work. She has blessed us with a blueprint for belonging."

—Dr. Paula Stone Williams, TED speaker and author of *As a Woman: What I Learned About Power, Sex, and the Patriarchy After I Transitioned*

"*Braving the Workplace* should be read, applied, and used to create joy! Beth's ideas, stories, and tools help me experience belonging by accepting myself, being vulnerable, and braving the workplace so that the workplace works for me."

—Dave Ulrich, Rensis Likert Professor at Ross School of Business, University of Michigan, and partner at The RBL Group

"Stop trying to fit in. You don't have to mold yourself into something you're not so that other people like you. It's time to be who YOU are and go after what you want. Let this book be your guide to get you there."

—Mel Robbins, bestselling author and host of *The Mel Robbins Podcast*

"*Braving the Workplace* is a must-read for anyone struggling to maintain equilibrium in an upside-down world. Which is pretty much all of us. Dr. Beth Kaplan shares practical coping skills augmented with stories that deepen her message. The book also includes handy self-assessments and thought-provoking questions that enable the reader to consider where they are now, what they may wish to change, and, if they change, how to get there."

—John Baldoni, member of 100 Coaches and author of many books, including *Grace Under Pressure: Leading Through Change and Crisis*

"In today's fast-paced world, authentic leadership is more critical than ever. *Braving the Workplace* isn't just another leadership book; it's a practical tool that helps leaders create environments where everyone feels valued and connected. It's not about grand pronouncements, but the daily actions that make a difference."

—Dr. Marshall Goldsmith, Thinkers50 #1 executive coach and New York Times bestselling author of *The Earned Life, Triggers, and What Got You Here Won't Get You There*

"If you've recently asked yourself, 'Am I truly happy at work? Am I my best self?' now is the time to do something about it. *Braving the Workplace* will give you everything you need."

—Adrian Gostick, #1 *New York Times* bestselling author of *The Carrot Principle, Culture Guru,* and host of the Anxiety at Work Podcast

"Dr. Beth Kaplan explores what it means to belong in the modern work environment. Every C-Suite executive needs to understand and define the next era of workplace dynamics. Dr. Kaplan's ability to blend research with actionable, executive-level insights is an accelerant to transforming workplaces for the better."

—Brian Solis, world-renowned digital anthropologist, futurist, and head of global innovation at ServiceNow

"*Braving the Workplace* is an essential read for leaders who recognize the value of seeing employees as whole individuals. Dr. Kaplan expertly illustrates how a culture of belonging builds a supportive environment where people feel truly valued and connected. This book is a powerful guide for creating workplaces that not only drive success but also elevate the human experience."

—John Spence, global thought leader in business and leadership

"Beth Kaplan's *Braving the Workplace* is essential reading for today's work environment, offering practical tips to achieve success while prioritizing mental health. It encourages viewing jobs as actions, not just titles, fostering a balanced and fulfilling career. Highly recommended for anyone seeking workplace success and well-being."

—Michael Levitt, chief burnout officer at Breakfast Leadership Network

"Dr. Beth Kaplan's insightful book, *Braving the Workplace*, is a must-read for many audiences but perhaps most especially for corporate managers. Historical and generational trends in belonging, identity, and work-life balance are not just explained here but pieced together like a jigsaw puzzle that forms the roadmap for a corporate culture that can perform without sacrificing self. Dr. Kaplan brilliantly weaves in her own personal stories, self-tests for the readers, and offers antidotes from a lifetime of considered thought on the complex topic of belonging."

—Anthony Costello, CEO of Medidata

"Beth has achieved something truly transformative in this book. She has not only shared her deeply personal journey but also managed to turn her lived experience into a normative guide that can inspire and empower a wide readership. Though not lengthy, this book is a powerful and vibrant testament to the potential for change at work and in life. Her ultimate aim is to make work work better than it does now. She wants the workplace to take people and their whole selves into account. She acknowledges that work is not only part of life but a significant and enduring part of life. A great work experience has impact way beyond the workplace, and a poor, negative work experience can destroy one's sense of self. Beth is unshrinkingly confrontational with herself. She looks at herself and her life experiences in the mirror and is unblinkingly honest. She turns this honesty into positive energy and ensures that everything she says resonates beyond her experience. This builds into the final chapter, where she discusses the workforce, work, and what needs to be done to make the workplace decent, more human, and resonant. Beth points out how important work is for our identities and self-belief. She also forcibly points out that we are all bigger than our jobs, and if we define ourselves by our jobs, we miss out on the rich bonus of bringing our whole selves to work. This is an essential message. If you work for a company that denies you the opportunity to be yourself, the outcome is clear: find someone or an employer who will allow you to do that. Your life will be richer and more fulfilling, and you will be more productive and creative as a result."

—Dr. Nigel Paine, co-presenter at Learning Now TV and bestselling author of *The Learning Challenge, Building Leadership Development Programmes that Work,* and *Workplace Learning: How to Build a Culture of Continuous Employee Development*

"Who plays the most pivotal role in employee belonging and psychological safety? The simple but profound answer is managers. Their impact has spillover effects into employees' lives. Beth Kaplan explains in detail why this is true and in *Braving the Workplace* offers ideas and practices for becoming a great manager."

—Amy C Edmondson, Novartis Professor of Leadership at Harvard Business School and author of *Right Kind of Wrong: The Science of Failing Well*

Braving the Workplace

Braving the Workplace

Belonging at the Breaking Point

by Dr. Beth Kaplan, Ed.D.

MIAMI

For permission requests, please contact the publisher at:
Mango Publishing Group
5966 South Dixie Highway, Suite 300
Miami, FL 33143
info@mango.bz

For special orders, quantity sales, course adoptions and corporate sales, please
email the publisher at sales@mango.bz. For trade and wholesale sales, please
contact Ingram Publisher Services at customer.service@ingramcontent.com or
+1.800.509.4887.

Braving the Workplace: Belonging at the Breaking Point

Library of Congress Cataloging-in-Publication number: 2024943931
ISBN: (print) 978-1-68481-695-8, (ebook) 978-1-68481-696-5
BISAC category code: BUS118000, BUSINESS & ECONOMICS / Diversity & Inclusion
https://drbethkaplan.com/home/

To Steve, Joshua, & Owen—my boys with the biggest hearts with the greatest abundance for love who fill my bucket every day.

A Note from the Author

I know what it's like to be unseen, unheard, and unhappy. I know what it's like to feel so much and have so much to say but you can't find the words to express what you are going through. I know what it's like to feel tired, a deep fatigue preventing you from absorbing joy. It's lonely. But you are not alone. We're in this together.

The good news is that you've survived 100 percent of your toughest days and I will get you through the rest.

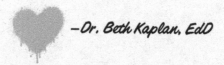 —Dr. Beth Kaplan, EdD

Table of Contents

Foreword by Jean Kantambu Latting, DrPH, LMSW

In this heartfelt and illuminating book, Dr. Beth Kaplan shares her personal journey of discovery, guiding us through the vital importance of belonging in our workplaces and personal lives, while offering compassionate insights and practical wisdom for navigating our own paths.

She opens the book with a powerful promise to the reader:

> I know what it's like to be unseen, unheard, and unhappy. I know what it's like to feel so much and have so much to say but you can't find the words to express what you are going through. I know what it's like to feel tired, a deep fatigue, preventing you from absorbing joy. It's lonely. But you are not alone. We're in this together. The good news is that you've survived 100% of your toughest days and I am going to get you through the rest.

Indeed, Dr. Kaplan fulfills this promise. Through stories of her own life and references to both popular and scholarly authors, she explains why she became interested enough in the topic of belonging to commit her time and effort to writing about it. However, most impressive is Dr. Kaplan's groundbreaking academic research throughout the book and how she translates behavioral science into everyday practices we all can use. It is no wonder that she is considered one of the world's leading experts on belonging.

Dr. Kaplan's compelling narrative of her ultimately futile attempts to achieve belonging in an unforgiving workplace resonated deeply with me. It accurately captures what people, myself included, go through in places where they are told in multiple ways that they don't belong.

Like many others, I stayed in a workplace where I felt misaligned, undervalued, and undermined. It wasn't until several friends bluntly told me that I was in an untenable situation that I was able to step outside of myself and realize I had to take a stand on my own behalf.

Dr. Kaplan aims to spare readers this form of self-devaluing and torture. She wants readers in such situations to have sufficient knowledge and examples that they can recognize what is happening to them, and not think a superhuman effort will pull them through —or feel like a failure if, despite their best efforts, they are still put outside the insiders' circle.

She explains key concepts such as belonging, inclusivity, bravery, and courage, distinguishing among them and highlighting their importance. She discusses the crucial role of managers in setting the tone and culture of a workplace and how to recognize toxic environments.

Throughout the book, Dr. Kaplan provides questionnaires and tools for readers to assess themselves and determine the level of isolation —or even danger—they might be in. One critical clue is whether the stress is threatening their own mental and physical health. She doesn't shy away from the term "suicide ideation" as one possible outcome if a person submits to an unrelenting work environment.

Toward the end, she offers a framework for deciding whether to stay or leave a job, with the bottom line questions being: Are your values aligned with the organization, or are they misaligned? Is your health being jeopardized if you stay? Are you growing or stagnant? Can you support the organization fully with your whole, authentic self, and does it support you in return?

As a leadership coach specializing in diversity, equity, and inclusion, I found this book truly eye-opening. Before my in-depth conversation with Kaplan and reading her insights, I hadn't fully realized how important it is to distinguish between belonging and inclusion. This book changed my mind: inclusion is something the organization provides, while belonging is the impact on the individual—whether the person feels a sense of connection, acceptance, and being valued.

When we stay in environments where we believe we don't belong, we put ourselves at risk.

Dr. Kaplan's stance in this book is clear: she understands why people stay in challenging work situations, but her fervent wish is for readers to use this book to reevaluate their circumstances and leave if necessary. To that end, the book provides an opportunity for readers to track their origin stories, put their pasts in perspective, identify what's important to them, recognize their areas of strength, and gain perspective on their current situation.

In essence, Dr. Kaplan's work serves as both a mirror and a guide, helping readers recognize unhealthy work environments and providing them with the tools to make informed decisions about their professional and personal lives. It's a valuable resource for anyone struggling with workplace belonging, offering both empathy and practical advice for navigating your challenging situations.

Chapter 1
Where Do I Belong?

True story: I've never felt like I belonged. Anywhere. For a long time, I felt bad about that. Like an outsider looking in. Now, don't get me wrong, sometimes in life I feel connected to friends and connected to something bigger than myself. But those times typically have come with me sacrificing a part of myself to fit in. This is a pattern I see going way back. I had friends but I didn't let them in. I had a family that actively made me the black sheep so I went with it. I was so uncomfortable in my skin, but to the outside world, I seemingly had it all.

Family is the first community that impacts our sense of "belonging." However, I was raised in a dysfunctional household, and my sense of safety and belonging were disrupted. I never let anyone know this, not even my closest friends, because I was ashamed. I felt unworthy of love and was afraid that if they found out that my family deemed me unlovable, they would see me as unlovable too.

I craved familial love, and you can imagine that when I got married and had my first child, I believed that it was finally happening. On top of those milestones, I started a new job, working for my dream company. I interviewed with them and one of their values was family. Can you hear the harps playing in the background? I did. I felt like it was all meant to be. About two weeks into my tenure there, my son was diagnosed with lung cancer at two months old. It is the worst pain I've ever felt. I wanted to die. The uncertainty, the knowledge that my sweet boy's life may be over before it began. It was all too much. At the time, doctors told us that going five years without symptoms and a return of cancer was our initial goal. I prayed for life to fast forward to the five-year mark.

My son had chemotherapy for the first eighteen months of his life, and I sunk into a harrowing depression. I struggled to breathe daily. Seeing my sweet boy, barely out of the newborn phase, so innocent and sick beyond belief: No one should have to go through it. During that time, I was faced with caring for a sick child and the uncertainty of his fragile life, and my husband and I started to notice our friend group dwindling. It's not like you see it on TV where the community wraps their arms around you, at least not the way we experienced it. People didn't know what to say, so they stopped reaching out, and we felt isolated. I think the term is "cancer ghosting"—when people cut contact or communication with you after a cancer diagnosis. It's pretty counterintuitive, am I right? Cancer should be a time when friends and family come together full of love and support—at least that is what I thought would happen. It didn't.

As our community started to dwindle, I had a lot of time to sit with myself, to take a deeper look at me, and oh yeah, experience extreme discomfort. For eighteen months, while being terrified of my son dying and losing most people around me, I was stuck with myself, forced to sit with my pain and sadness. I was afraid to leave the house and bring germs back into it. I was nervous that people would continue to ghost us, so I stopped telling people. My one safe space was work. No one there knew what I was going through. it's impossible to ghost us if you don't know about the cancer. Sounded logical to me. You are probably thinking, *how is that possible?* How did no one at work know what my family was going through? I was good at covering up what was going on with my life. To be honest, they never asked, so I never shared. My managers didn't get to know me, or I may have cracked and let them into my world. But that didn't happen, and I embraced the workplace, justifying my silence with the notion that for eight or nine hours every day, in between taking care of a sick child, I got to feel normal and not obsessively think about cancer.

Okay, moment of truth. There will be a lot of people that know me and may be hearing for the first time that my son was born with cancer. It's not something you casually slide into a conversation, and even now, writing the words, it's hard to breathe and I may be bawling my eyes out getting my computer wet with tears. Of the people I did tell, I no longer talk to 80 percent of them—and if I didn't tell you, it's most likely related to the whole getting ghosted thing. It hurt. Bad. When I needed them the most.

So why now? Why tell the world? 1) My son gave me his permission (since it's his truth to tell), and 2) I want to help other people. Looking back, this time in life and all of the awful discomfort made me take a true, hard look at myself, and while this was the worst experience of my life, it started my quest for true belonging. My struggles gave me a new perspective and boy, did I search for it. All of the suffering needed to mean something. It's at this time that I fell in love with how Brené Brown described belonging. She said that belonging is about being part of something bigger than ourselves, requiring us to "believe in and belong to ourselves so fully that we can find sacredness both in being a part of something and in standing alone when necessary." [1]

Fifteen years later and my son is in remission. I can proudly say that despite the challenges my life has never been the same. Without my struggles, comedies, and tragedies, I may have never gotten to know myself and felt comfortable in my own skin. At first, I credited my success to my job, this "family" that embraced me. About five years in, I started to question whether I was truly being myself at work. If I couldn't be my authentic self, did my coworkers really know me? What was I sacrificing to be the "Beth" they saw every day—the one everyone considered a "work superstar"?

In the working world, I was on a roll, a steep upward trajectory. I was winning accolades, getting promoted easily, and eventually, I ran sales onboarding for one of the most successful organizations in the world, welcoming more than fifteen thousand new hires a year. I was the motherfucking cheerleader welcoming you into "the family" and I loved it. I loved my team, new hires, and that feeling of creating this nirvana of workplaces. I was stirring the Kool-Aid in the backroom and rolling it out for happy hour and my world felt like not only were we indoctrinating people into the culture, but that we were the culture. Finally, after such hard, hard years, I was winning. It was intoxicating, and by all definitions, I felt like maybe this was where I belonged until one day, my manager left, and she'd been my pal, my partner, my work bestie. My new skip-level manager, not so much. He didn't get along with my manager that left and by default, didn't take to me from the start. It felt very "guilty until proven innocent." Great.

This new manager was beloved in the company. I was excited to work with him, but it was unrequited. I was part of something larger than me, but I had to sacrifice who I was to be me at work; the work version—and my newfound sense of belonging—went out the window as I tried harder and harder to get in good with the new manager. I was confused 90 percent of the time and filled with negative, scary thoughts. This was a family, and it also supported my family. Why was no one else feeling this way? I kept my feelings inside; I didn't want to stand out, so I kept going—after all, as they say in the navy, "Ship, shipmate, self," right?

Performance evaluation time came, and my manager called me into his office. He said, "Beth, you are my top employee; you do an amazing job, but you don't belong here." For the next two minutes, I felt like he was the teacher from Charlie Brown. That "wah, wah, wah" was all I could make out. Once I came to, he said he had a meeting to go to, but we'd catch up soon.

Over the next few months, I worked hard to win him over at great cost to myself. I worked longer hours, often going to bed around two in the morning. To keep up, I was eating more, exercising less, and giving up any social life I had to prove my worth to my manager. I let him define my worth, and since he treated me like crap, I believed I was crap. Everyone around me was concerned. My hair was falling out, I was gaining weight, I removed myself from family and friends. I isolated myself, became depressed, and I felt worthless.

I thought to myself, *I will win him over.* The thought of someone not liking me, especially my manager, was too much to bear. I was a remote employee (before it was cool) and thought, *maybe he just doesn't know me well enough; maybe telling him more about me would help. That's it.* I just needed to be more vulnerable. If this were a movie, it would be a horror flick—the kind where the stupid kids stumble across an old, abandoned building and the audience is screaming, "No, don't go in," but the kids go in and they of course meet a horrible demise. That's right; that was me. In the spirit of him liking me once he knew me better, I felt like I needed to stop hiding; it was time. In our next one-on-one, I told my manager about my son's cancer. I instantly regretted it. I felt like a sell-out and guess what? It was for nothing. Not one thing changed. I don't remember him reacting other than to tell me he had a meeting to get to. The truth did not set me free; in fact, I sank even deeper into depression and self-loathing.

I worked harder and harder, trying to get somewhere with my manager. My mid-year performance review came about, and I met with my manager who told me that he appreciated my efforts and that while I was kicking ass, he found me to be the type of person who achieved amazing results because I was "leaving bodies in my wake." I started crying, uncontrollably crying, and I burst out how awful I'd been feeling. What I said next still haunts me. I told my manager something I had yet to even admit to myself. I told him i was suicidal. His reaction: crickets. Utter and complete silence. In what felt like a year later he said, "Glad to see you cry; it lets me know you have some range of emotion. Sorry, I have to go to my next meeting." Sucker punch. I gave it my all and it would never be enough. Never.

There is so much to say about this, and we have chapters and chapters to dive in. The *Reader's Digest* version of what followed: I quit, six months later, but I quit. As scared as I was before, quitting was brutal. I loved that company, I loved my team, and my entire identity was wrapped up in work. Even though I quit, the trauma of my experience followed me for years. The real work began, learning who I was and getting myself back. I did a lot of time with what Brené Brown would call "*embracing the suck.*"[2]

The good news: I went back to being the lovable rebel I'd always been. The even better news? I now embrace discomfort and rise in opposition to all of the "shoulds." You know, the shoulds: I should be thin, rich, pretty. Fuck the shoulds. (I curse a lot...might as well tell you now while we are getting to know each other.) I've learned a lot, and I will share it with you, starting with this: the hardest thing I needed to do after "embracing the suck" was to fight like hell to get myself back and remember who I am, not other people's perception of who I am.

Here's the thing: knowing ourselves is incredibly difficult. I mean, truly knowing ourselves is a lifelong journey and the reality is, it's a lot easier for you to be happy when you feel like you don't need to sacrifice who you are for anyone or anything. To know what you won't sacrifice you need to know who you are. Do you know who you are?

A phrase like that fifteen years ago would have made me slam this book shut and never pick it up again, staring at it from time to time as I used it to cover up a spot on my coffee table. Why? I couldn't be alone with myself. I was disgusted and scared as hell—about everything and I didn't even know why. Hell, I didn't know who I was beyond a mom with a newborn child with cancer. Five-plus years ago, I had no clue who I was, only that I didn't want to be here anymore. It was time to figure out who I was and now it's your turn too.

Your Personal Memo

Use this space to explore and articulate who you are. This memo is not a list of your accomplishments or achievements. While they are great, this is more of a focused memo that you will use to understand more of who you are.

Here are some things to consider:

- Be mindful of the relationship between yourself and your goals. This is meant to be about who you are, less so about your aspirational self...that will come later.

- Be sure to include the assumptions that shape who you've become.

- Feel free to add root cause details, beliefs, and ideologies that have shaped you.

- Note your biases and the potential implications/influences on what makes you, you.

And remember, we are in this together. In fact, my personal memo is below after yours. Read it before or after, whatever helps you most.

On paper, I am:

_____

_____

_____

Who I really am:

_____

_____

_____

Who I would like to be:

_____

_____

_____

Your origin story (ex: who did I want to be when I grew up? How and why I did or didn't become who I wanted when I grew up; who I lived with; what shaped me):

_____

_____

_____

_____

_____

_____

_____

_____

_____

_____

_____

_____

_____

_____

_____

_____

_____

_____

_____

_____

_____

_____

_____

My top five values:

_____

_____

_____

_____

_____

Two mottos I live by:

_____

_____

Biggest grudges—and why:

_____

_____

_____

_____

_____

My superpowers:

_____

_____

What I wish I did better:

_____

_____

_____

What keeps me up at night:

_____

_____

_____

What I want to remember coming away from this memo:

_____

_____

_____

And now, my personal memo.

On paper, I am: a wife, mother, daughter, sister, friend, doctor, academic, researcher, a Philly girl, short, super pale.

Who I really am: a mommy (not a mom), a loyal friend, a recovering people pleaser, a lovable rebel, a fighter, a grudge-holder.

What I would like to be: patient, forgiving, a member of a big group of friends.

Your origin story: As a young child, I grew up in a lower-middle-class suburb of Philadelphia. I lived with my mom, dad, and sister. My dad was diagnosed with multiple sclerosis (MS) before I was born and he got sicker as I started elementary school. It was hard for my parents to make ends meet. When my mother became the main provider, I became a caregiver to my younger sister and at times, my dad. The parent-child dynamic changed, and my role conflict manifested in both emotional ways that left me confused and lonely.

I had little escape and so I became an avid reader and dreamer. I wanted to be a singer and actress. When I told my mom, she laughed and told me that I would never make it. It's the first time I remember looking at her and crying. She told me I was meant to be a lawyer. I later went to college to be a lawyer and found out I didn't want to be a lawyer. I waited two full years to tell my mom and she told me I was a disappointment. At age twenty, this was my first true act of rebellion, with many more acts to follow.

Developing friendships in childhood was hard but doable as long as they didn't know what was happening at home. It was hard to be my true self. I felt that I lived in the shadow of a sick parent and a mother who always valued her friends over me. I was fearful so much so that I spent all of the third grade silent in school and developed a nervous cough. I was scared of my own voice. It could be from my mom telling me that the words coming out of my mouth sounded stupid, the deep belonging uncertainty that I was going through, or the fear of my dad dying (I started to learn more about MS).

The year I turned eleven, I went to an overnight camp where I experienced independence, self-esteem, and confidence for the first time. That confidence flowed into middle school where I made friends, ran for class vice president, joined team sports, and overall, I became more of a risk-taker. As the years went by, I applied to attend global programs to start exploring the world. At age fifteen, I attended the March of the Living, an annual educational program that brings students from around the world to Poland and then Israel to explore the remnants of the Holocaust. After that experience, I felt a responsibility to keep learning and saw my education as a gift. I was grouped with kids from around the world and the experience gave me an appreciation for different cultures and ways of living.

After March of the Living, I was hooked on travel and applied to as many programs that offered scholarships as possible. Living with kids from around the globe gave me a taste for diversity, inclusion, collaboration, and community service. It also gave me the confidence to become more independent and taught me that sometimes the greatest gift you can give another person is to include them.

Social interactions and having a lot of friends were paramount to my mom. When I hit high school and used to roll in packs of twenty, that's when I think she was most proud of me. But I was always a little lost. I thought that friendship was pleasing people, and letting my guard down would expose why they would not want to be friends with me. I carried a lot of fear and shame.

My top five values: love, family, gratitude, learning, and integrity. Damn, that was hard. I could have easily named twenty.

Two mottos I live by:

- Leave people better than you found them.

- Be bold in what you stand for and be careful what you fall for.

Biggest grudges—and why:

- Any friend that has dissed me when they "find a better deal." That feeling is too much for me.

- Narcissistic behavior is a deal-breaker. I absorb others' emotions. My deep desire to help leaves me feeling drained, overwhelmed, and vulnerable to their manipulation, demands, and lack of reciprocity—and who likes being taken advantage of? Not me. I no longer make time for that bullshit.

- Anyone who is not awesome to my kids when they meet them or underestimates them—immediate grudge, maybe for life. Are they perfect? One hundred percent, no. Are they my everything? One hundred percent, yes! If standing up for my kids burns bridges, I'll supply the matches.

My superpowers: I'm great at helping others, giving from my heart. I'm a kick-ass friend. I'm an excellent sleeper. I'm a great problem-solver. I'm good at bringing out the best in others. I'm thoughtful. My intuition is solid.

What I wish I did better: *so much*, but I will be gentle with myself on this one! I wish I had better boundaries and that I was clear and upfront about them. I wish I was better at noticing quality over quantity in friendships. I wish I was patient.

What keeps me up at night: I worry about the health and happiness of my family and try to do my best for them. I worry about getting this book completed.

What I want to remember coming away from this memo: I've come a long way from the girl who was afraid to speak out loud for fear of sounding stupid. I'm not broken; I'm human.

Congratulations—that was a big step in understanding yourself. For me, it was hard (most things worth doing are). What I did next, I highly advise you to do the same. Grab a highlighter or pen and start to mark themes and patterns that you see repeating.

What did you notice? Did you see any themes and patterns that help explain your way of being? Your sense of belonging? When I highlighted and circled, my themes felt like a flashing neon sign, but I didn't know how to read what they were telling me. I didn't see my diagnosis coming even though I've made a career out of it. It didn't matter that I specialized in the exact thing that I struggled with; I didn't realize that what I suffered from was a lack of and often thwarted belonging. Here are a couple of the themes I noted:

1. I have a pattern of issues stemming from childhood and what shaped me called disorganized/disoriented attachment (from psychologist Mary Ainsworth's 1978 attachment theory), described as:[3]

    - fearful, emotionally overwhelmed, and distressed for long periods of time;

    - without a clear strategy for dealing with their distress;

    - sees caregivers and the world as dangerous and unpredictable;

    - sees themselves as bad or unworthy of love and care.

    Sound familiar to you? Do you recognize any of these patterns too? Well, a feeling of belonging and connection can foster the ability to enjoy secure attachment in a safe and accepting environment. Children with disorganized/ disoriented attachment have a hard time experiencing belonging. This makes a lot of sense to me. I was eager to please, to be needed, to feel like I mattered, to fit in anywhere, and I was flooded by fear of neglect and abuse. So, it makes sense why I have loyalty and abandonment issues now and have been confused about the meaning of belonging for pretty much forever.

2. My grudges stem from my mommy issues. Never feeling good enough, I will not let that happen again. Likewise, it is most likely why I overdo it with being a mama bear.

3. For most of my life, I've suffered from not feeling like I
    belonged. I never realized that belonging was more about
    feeling okay with me, belonging to myself. In fact, I tried to
    be anything but me, to be liked and to fit in somewhere and,
    as a result, I tried to attach to anything that would have me,
    or give positive reinforcement, or that thought I was lovable.
    That lack of belonging is called thwarted belonging, and we'll
    dive into that plenty in this book.

Suffering from lack of belonging or thwarted belonging isn't
necessarily a diagnosis, but it should be. A strong sense of
belonging is a predictor of good health and when a sense of
belonging is not met or thwarted, it is causal to loneliness and
depression. We get diagnosed with depression and anxiety,
and we talk about belonging as an antecedent of a disordered
environment and experiences. But what if it's more than an
antecedent and it's the outcome? After all, we are hardwired to
belong. We need it to survive, it's essential, and a lack of belonging
is like a lack of food and water.

While I believe that a lack of belonging is its own diagnosis, it
is important to note that thwarted belonging is also a strong
predictor of suicide. Psychologist and suicide expert Thomas
Joiner's 2005 interpersonal theory of suicide postulates that
suicidal impulses arise when individuals experience uncontrollable
feelings of self-perceived burdensomeness accompanied by a
thwarted sense of belonging.[4] The United Nations reports that
one in a hundred deaths is by suicide, making it a leading cause of
death worldwide. With this epidemic on the rise, doctors have a
responsibility to get to the root causes and act by diagnosing and
treating the lack of belonging. So, I ask again, why aren't doctors
diagnosing it and treating it?

When I was at my all-time low after my son was diagnosed with cancer, I brought my pain and struggles to my doctor and she said, "Maybe you need to go out and make friends." To her, belonging was about membership. Her response sent me into a tailspin as I assumed that there was something wrong with me that I could control. Like if I had more friends I wouldn't struggle. I tried that; it didn't work, and ultimately, I felt like a failure. But was it my failure? Or was it the failure of my doctor to diagnose my lack of belonging and treat it as a condition needing mental health help? Why aren't doctors and psychologists treating thwarted or impaired belonging as a diagnosis? Let's dive in to understand belonging and make a case for the change we need to see in the world of belonging psychology.

Belonging is a complex concept. Ask ten people what belonging means and you will get ten different answers. Just like my doctor thought it was membership, others believe it is fitting in, or inclusion, or diversity, or attachment. How do we distinguish one assumption from the next? It seems like belonging is this big lump: you belong or you don't belong, or we used to belong and now we don't. It's a more complex phenomenon than that. In an ideal world, belonging is a happy feeling, but when belonging goes awry or belonging uncertainty sets in it leads to negative effects like thwarted belonging—then, our sense of belonging can be crippling. Before we dive into the impact of belonging, let's level set on what belonging is and is not.

The Reset on *Belonging*

It's no wonder why people are so confused when they hear the word *belonging*. When you look at the etymology of the word *belonging*, here is what you get.

belong (v.)

mid-14c., "to go along with, properly relate to," from be-
intensive prefix, + longen "to go," from Old English langian
"pertain to, to go along with," which is of uncertain origin but
perhaps related to the root of long (adj.). Senses of "be the
property of" and "be a member of" first recorded late 14c.

As the language evolved to Middle English, unfortunately
belonging did not evolve with it. *Be-* + *longen* or *belonging* meant
"to be fitting, be suitable." Thus, belonging was associated with
membership and fitting in...even worse maybe, being good enough
to be suitable for membership. So, the deal was, you belonged as
long as you were accepted for being like everyone else.

In *Braving the Wilderness* (an excellent read), Brené Brown
defines belonging as: "the innate human desire to be part of
something larger than us," and she contends that **true belonging**
is experienced when people present their authentic selves,
achieving a level of self-acceptance.[5] I agree and want to up the
ante. I define *belonging* as the innate human desire to be part of
something larger than us **without sacrificing who we are**. Okay,
yes, I know some sacrifice is virtuous, like sacrificing service for
country, but the kind of sacrifice I am talking about here is neither
honorable nor noble; it is consuming and dangerous. Self-sacrifice
is a tricky thing. On the surface, it doesn't seem like a bad thing—
after all, you are helping others and may feel kind and selfless at
the time. Some people call it being generous, but make no mistake,
sometimes you can be so helpful to others that it becomes
hurtful to yourself. Without limitations, we tend to self-sacrifice
to a chronic level, to our own dysfunction, valuing others over
ourselves. So, in adding this note about sacrifice in the definition
of belonging, we remind ourselves to be careful of our level of
sacrifice so that we don't overdo it to our own detriment and
experience thwarted belonging.

Thwarted belonging occurs when a sense of belonging is not met.
What causes belonging not to be met? Two credible psychologists
and researchers, Roy Baumeister and Mark Leary, believed that
thwarted belonging is caused by social exclusion and rejection
which causes self-regulation and intelligent thought to be
impaired.[6] More recently, Thomas Joiner described thwarted
belonging as a psychologically painful mental state achieved when
a connection is unrequited, causing dread and fear among other
emotions.[7] So, all the experts believe that thwarted belonging
occurs when social connection is not achieved. *This* expert is
here to respectfully add a layer to how we think about thwarted
belonging. In addition to social rejection, thwarted belonging
occurs when you don't feel good about yourself, to a crippling
degree. So, if you don't feel like yourself and the consequences
are dire, if you feel like you are burdensome, unlovable, and like
you don't fit into your own skin, that is thwarted belonging. But if
you are looking for a more formal definition: thwarted belonging
occurs when a sense of belonging is not met **due to rejection of self
by self and/or others**. What other people think of you is one thing,
but what you think of yourself is most important, and without
belonging to yourself you can't actualize belonging to something
larger than yourself.

While we are on a roll with these definitions, you may be asking
yourself, *is that it?* Nope, here are two others: **sacrificial belonging**
and **dissimulated belonging**.

Sacrificial belonging occurs when one consciously or
subconsciously gives up what they value, including their physical
and mental health, for the sake of meeting expectations, believing
that this disequilibrium equates to an authentic experience of
belonging. Sacrificial belonging is a negative sense of belonging
that is not quite thwarted. In fact, to the person engaging in
sacrificial acts, their behavior may seem positive but there are

always negative outcomes when giving up any aspect of what makes you, you for the sake of something else. It reminds me of the Horcrux from the *Harry Potter* books. In this fictitious yet all too familiar world, a Horcrux is an object in which a dark wizard or witch hides a fragment of his or her soul to become immortal. The Horcrux is the most terrible of all dark magic. In fact, Horcruxes can only be created after committing the supreme act of evil— murder—and are a means to tear the soul.[8] Sacrificing who you are, similar to when we fragment our identities, tears apart our souls.

You may be thinking, *that's awful, who would do that?* Many employees in the corporate world have identified as experiencing sacrificial belonging. They said that they knowingly suffer because they believe the work or company is worth all of their effort and sacrifice, as if there are equal properties being traded: the sense and identity of the self for belonging to an organization, their soul for a Horcrux, tenure and belonging to a company. They liken themselves to athletes and see this as improving their performance. Yet where athletes have coaches and trainers protecting them from this kind of dangerous erosion of self, employees do not have a similar safety net and can easily be taken advantage of by managers who may be more preoccupied with achieving corporate goals than protecting the people who work for them. Does it ever end well?

Dissimulated belonging occurs when one does not feel a sense of belonging but pretends that they do or disconnects from an environment (like the workplace) on purpose. The still may have a sense of belonging; it just may not derive from said environment. You may ask, is that the same as covering? Close, but no cigar. Covering is a term coined by sociologist and social psychologist Erving Goffman in 1963 as a form of identity management in which individuals hide, downplay, or disassociate from one of their identities of race, gender, or sexual orientation. [9]

One example of this is when people try to fit in—which is the opposite of belonging because if you have to cover up who you are or change it to be accepted, that is not true belonging. Now, typically, people try to fit in because they want to belong to something, but other times people try to fit in as a means to an end or a way to get people off their backs. For example, people may try to belong to a social group to make their social standing easier. Let's take my friend Rory. Rory hates running; however, she goes running with a group of ladies every morning because she doesn't want to miss out on the gossip. The girls she runs with think she loves running, but she likes the connection and interaction, and she sucks up the running part to be part of the group.

If dissimulated belonging is not *covering*, how about *masking*? Still no. Masking is more commonly associated with complete concealment or alteration of one's identity or true self. It often implies a more thorough and sometimes more psychologically taxing effort to hide one's true feelings, thoughts, or characteristics. Masking is frequently discussed in the context of neurodiverse individuals, such as those with autism, who may mask their symptoms or behaviors to blend in with neurotypical peers. So, not the same.

The most common question I get is: *is dissimulated belonging a positive or negative?* I believe it is positive because people with dissimulated belonging still experience a positive sense of belonging—it just doesn't come from one source. Belonging is not an all-nothing concept and the more we preach that belonging is derived from one place, the workplace, it will have an adverse impact. People who don't feel like they belong to a workplace may feel that they don't belong anywhere. Here's the thing about dissimulated belonging: the only people who usually have a problem with it are the people around dissimulated belongers because they can't fathom to believe the workplace doesn't supply everyone with their prime sense of belonging. The workplace has become a place that values company cheerleaders and where a workplace mission becomes a personal mission. Dissimulated belongers get their purpose outside of the workplace. That's okay—actually, it is more than okay; it is positive and healthy.

Next most common question: *does that mean that dissimulated is true belonging?* Belonging is not all or nothing—so it can be true as well as dissimulated. True belonging fosters genuine connections and acceptance. Dissimulating belonging is not sacrificing who we are. Dissimulated belonging, while involving some adjustments, can be a strategic way for individuals to navigate complex social environments and gradually build deeper, more authentic connections over time.

What Belonging Is Not

We talked a lot about what belonging is and different types of belonging. How about what it's not? Belonging is not about fitting in. Fitting in means changing the way you act, speak, behave to conform to someone's way of being—sacrificing yourself and what makes you, you. Belonging is a feeling that you determine for yourself, and while fitting in may be an action you perform, it requires acceptance by others. Belonging is about being true to yourself, while fitting in is about being what everyone else needs. I'm a Philly girl and when I go to a bar and see an Eagles or 76ers fan (try not to hold this against me), I immediately gravitate to them. Why? Because I don't have to be anyone except myself with them, we like the same things, and they will like me because we share teams. This is me being authentic to myself and others appreciating me for who I am. It's me being part of something larger than myself and not giving up what makes me, me.

Belonging is not membership. While membership is certainly a component of belonging, true belonging goes beyond mere inclusion or affiliation with a group. Membership refers to the formal or informal process of joining a group or community, and it is a basic requirement for feeling a sense of belonging within that group. People may confuse belonging and membership because membership is often a prerequisite for a community or larger group where we may seek belonging. For example, to feel like you belong to a particular club or organization, you typically have to become a member first. Similarly, to feel like you belong to a particular social group, you need to be accepted by its members and be considered a part of the group. However, membership alone is not enough to create a sense of belonging. Belonging involves feeling a deep connection within the group, not just meeting the criteria for being a member.

People may confuse belonging and membership because our society often places a strong emphasis on belonging to groups and institutions to find meaning and identity. This can lead to a focus on the external markers of belonging. Examples include membership cards or group affiliations, rather than the internal experience of feeling connected, accepted, valued, and cared for that one may use to evaluate their sense of belonging.

When Belonging Is Not Met

When belonging is not met, what happens? A lack of belonging hurts our ability to thrive. Couple that with belonging uncertainty and it can sometimes feel like we are losing our minds. Negative belonging experiences can turn positive behaviors into conditions linked to mental and physical illnesses. This makes sense since the need to belong is hardwired in our DNA, and when brains sense rejection or exclusion, neural and physiological patterns like physical pain can occur. The negative response we feel when a lack of belonging sets in is part of our "neural alarm system," which protects against the isolating consequences of social separation and a variety of ill effects on health, adjustment, and well-being. The term "neural alarm system" is interpreted to refer to the brain's response to potentially threatening or dangerous situations, which involves a complex network of neural pathways and circuits that detect, process, and respond to incoming sensory information.

The neural alarm system is often referred to as the "fight or flight" response and is triggered by the activation of the sympathetic nervous system. This results in a series of physiological changes, including increased heart rate, elevated blood pressure, rapid breathing, and heightened awareness, that help prepare the body for action in response to a perceived threat. The neural alarm system is an important survival mechanism that helps protect us from harm, but it can also be triggered in situations where there is no real danger, leading to feelings of anxiety or panic. Understanding how this system works can help us better manage our response to stress and anxiety and develop strategies for coping with challenging situations. This alarm system in the body starts to mentally and physically suffer, and like with any alarm clock, we sometimes hit snooze, and then the pain gets worse and worse. So, don't press snooze on yourself!

A host of health issues like loneliness, anxiety, depression, and physical aches and pains are real ailments stemming from a lack of belonging. In addition, participants in my research have told me they experienced sleeplessness, weight loss and weight gain, hair pulling, self-harm, and suicidal ideation (as did I) related to lack of belonging and belonging uncertainty. In addition to our minds being impaired, lack of belonging physically hurts us, something rarely talked about. As this pain permeates, additional consequences occur, such as deterioration and distortion of our working memory. Working memory is the system that helps us keep things in mind while performing complex tasks such as reasoning, comprehension, and learning. When our working memory is impaired, our ability to process high quantities of information is impacted. Your perception, the story you tell yourself, becomes a reality because even if one manages to remember information, the mental workspace may still be distorted, a.k.a. it feels like your memory is betraying you.

The way we interpret and make sense of the world around us can shape our experiences and outcomes. Our thoughts and beliefs have a powerful influence on our behavior and emotions. From a psychological perspective, our perceptions are influenced by a variety of factors, including our past experiences, cultural background, personal values, and cognitive biases. These factors shape how we interpret events and situations, influencing our emotions and actions in response. The idea that our perceptions can shape our reality is also closely linked to the concept of self-fulfilling prophecies. This means that our beliefs and expectations about a situation can shape our behaviors and actions in ways that make those beliefs more likely to become reality. For example, if you believe that you are not good at public speaking, this belief may cause you to feel anxious and avoid opportunities to speak in public, which can further reinforce your belief and make it more difficult to overcome.

Another real and harmful impact we face is the aligned stigma associated with a lack of belonging and belonging uncertainty. Experts Gregory Walton and Geoffrey Cohen found that belonging uncertainty is a major contributing factor to the stigma associated with lack of belonging,[10] that repeatedly questioning whether we belong and inevitably facing setbacks and challenges result in diminished motivation and the belief that we can never succeed. This is particularly challenging since people are in constant self-evaluation mode, assessing who they are and where they belong, all to find and know themselves better. The weight of self-stigma leads to a heavy burden we put on ourselves: shame. An overload of shame, based on personal and societal expectations, amplifies uncertainty and undermines an individual's sense of belonging. All people experience a sense of shame, and while shame can be temporary, it can also manifest in a way that leads to the long-term erosion of confidence and self-worth. Shame can lead to dark impulses as we experience uncontrollable feelings of self-perceived burdensomeness and a thwarted sense of belonging accompanied by the capability for suicide. Yikes, it's bad.

Shame is perception-based, and perception is reality. For most of my life, I carried the shame of feeling unlovable. Why? When I was seventeen, my mom told me I was too hard to love. I was ashamed. I mean, whose mom can't love them? Therefore, I was unlovable. It took me twenty years to tell her how it made me feel and she didn't remember saying it at all.

So How Did We Get to This Place Where Belonging Got So Confusing?

People are in constant self-evaluation mode, assessing who they are and where they belong, all to find and know themselves better. One of the most important questions that we ask ourselves is, "Do I belong here?" In the search for this answer, it becomes about the quality of fit between oneself and the setting you are in. This

hasn't changed, so why are people so confused by the concept
of belonging?

In my research, it became apparent that there has been a major
shift over the last thirty to forty years in which people look to
the workplace for the feeling of belonging, a fit traditionally
experienced through family and tribes. Psychological needs
were initially met in the village community and religious rituals
started to be replaced by the institution of paid work as people
found themselves working more hours and gave up their leisure
time. As a result, the workplace expanded its scope, attempting
to foster belonging as shared beliefs to both keep up with socio-
cultural changes in the world and to improve bottom-line results,
particularly within the United States.

Another reason belonging became so confusing is the ongoing
belief that belonging is all or nothing. The age-old "you belong,
or you don't" simply isn't true. As time progresses and more and
more options are present, you can feel a sense of partial belonging,
belonging to parts of something but not all. You can also belong
to multiple communities at once. For example, I'm a member of
multiple women's professional networking groups. I pick what I
like about them, attending what I want and forgoing actions and
activities that don't serve me well. Gone are the days when you
need to be loyal to one group or one community only. Nowadays,
you can belong to parts of a community, many communities,
or none of the larger community depending on what matters
to you. For some, this is comforting—you want choices, you got
'em. For others, it can be scary, too much to navigate. For me,
it's comforting because growing up I felt like a freak. I thought
belonging was all or nothing and felt like such an oddball when
I didn't feel a sense of belonging to my community, my family. I
felt a sense of belonging with my grandparents and my sister but
not the rest of the members, which made me feel like an outcast.

Belonging can feel confusing when you start to think of all the shoulds that society puts on it.

Some may say that the concept of belonging started to get confusing when the world shut down due to the global COVID-19 pandemic. I'm going to call BS on that, and instead say our belonging epidemic was illuminated by the pandemic. We were lonely before the pandemic and isolated during the pandemic and that forced us to sit with ourselves and get to know ourselves better. But here we are, belonging in the age of loneliness. Surviving with the hope of thriving. What does it take to survive?

Chapter 2

Belonging and the Trauma-Informed State of the Workplace

The trouble with life is it doesn't come with a road map or an explicit itinerary of what you need to find your way home once you get yourself lost. This truism makes me think of Dorothy from *The Wizard of Oz*. She is far from home, following that circuitous and dangerous yellow brick road to get to the Emerald City, only to find out she possessed the power to get home via those fabulous ruby slippers that were on her feet the whole time.[11] Understanding our belongingness in the world is a similarly obstacle-strewn effort—whether that's navigating the roaring rivers of our family, avoiding conflict with our flying monkey friends, or allowing ourselves to surrender to a forever sleep in the metaphorical poppy fields of the workplace. Our search for a homecoming will only happen when we recognize how we hold the ruby slippers to our own belongingness story. But first...

Since we now look for belongingness in unfamiliar territories such as the workplace, it's important to understand the history of work and how we got here. If you're like me, you think about this at least once a week: Why did we settle on a five-day, forty-hour workweek? While Henry Ford is credited as one of the first employers to adopt a five-day, forty-hour week at his Ford Motor

Company plants in 1926,[12] the history of when we work and how much we work goes much deeper. So, buckle up.

Throughout history, how much people have worked both daily and weekly has drastically changed. For most of history, work hours were based on survival needs, religious traditions, and family life. For example, during the Stone Age, hunter-gatherers worked three to five hours a day, every day of the week, and their jobs were hunting and gathering food for sustenance, for survival. As early as 11,000 BCE, increasing population density and changes in climate created more demand for food than could be satisfied with hunting and gathering. This, along with increasing sophistication in food strategy, making agriculture more viable, led to a gradual transition away from a hunter-gatherer lifestyle toward cultivating crops and raising animals for food, and that led to working more hours a day, every day of the week.

Around 100 BCE, the average farmer worked eight hours a day, for about three hundred days a year.[13] Fast forward to medieval England where peasants typically worked from dusk until dawn. Work continued to get more exhausting in the seventeenth century where workers put in ten hours a day, 185 days a year, and a century later, workers averaged eleven-hour days, 208 days per year. Worse yet, nineteenth-century England workers averaged sixteen-hour days, 311 days a year.[14]

Crossing the pond in the nineteenth century, the work hours and days were just as aggressive if not more. With the Industrial Revolution, work skyrocketed beyond sixty hours a week. Workers put in six working days a week, and they worked an average of ten to twelve hours a day. In 1886, trade union members started to fight for a five-day, eight-hours-a-day working week, and reducing daily working hours. In most cases in the United States, Sunday was considered a day of rest, and eventually, Saturday as well so that more Americans could adhere to religious rules. Work came to a grinding halt with the Great Depression, where society settled at a five-day workweek and forty-hour workweek standard globally to reduce unemployment by distributing work more evenly among the available workforces.

While Henry Ford is credited with the work standard that we know today, the rich history of work goes back to the earliest stage of human civilization. Want to know something else that goes back to the earliest stage of human civilization? Belonging.

The New Place for Belonging

Since the Great Depression, society has kept the forty-hour workweek standard, but the concept and purpose of work have changed. Since the 1930s, there have been disruptions in people's traditional attachments that give rise to a sense of belonging. These disrupted attachments include territories (e.g., neighborhoods, motherland), social groups (e.g., religion), and political ideologies (e.g., socialism, feminism) that, individually or together, challenge a person's sense of belonging. Consequently, people are now turning to their workplace as a more stable attachment to nurture their fundamental need for belonging.

As the notions of family and religion have changed, so has the way that individuals look for meaning, purpose, and belonging. The notions of family and religion have indeed changed over time, as societal norms, values, and beliefs have evolved. In terms of family, there has been a shift from the traditional nuclear family structure, which consisted of a married couple and their children, to a more diverse range of family structures. Today, families can consist of single-parent households, blended families, same-sex parent households, and extended families that include grandparents, aunts, uncles, and cousins. This shift in family structure has been driven by several factors, including changing attitudes toward marriage and parenthood, advancements in reproductive technologies, and increased social acceptance of nontraditional family structures.

Similarly, the role of religion in society has also changed over time. In the past, religion played a more central role in many people's lives, with individuals and families often adhering to strict religious doctrines and participating in regular religious practices. Today, however, there has been a shift toward more secular values and beliefs, with many people identifying as spiritual but not religious or rejecting organized religion altogether. This shift has been driven by a few factors, including increased access to education and information, the rise of scientific rationalism, and changing cultural values.

Overall, the notions of family and religion have undergone significant changes over time, reflecting broader shifts in societal norms and values. As these shifts in family and religion have occurred, there have been changes in our traditions, rituals, and ways of socialization that typically occurred through the fabric of family, culture, and community where belonging may have been most associated. While structures and dynamics have changed, the need for meaning, justification, purpose, and even salvation has remained the same...we just look for them in different places now—in the workplace or our work in general.

People seek purpose and meaning in their work because, at our core, we all need to feel that our lives matter and that we're contributing to something bigger than ourselves—a true sense of belonging. Work takes up a significant portion of our time and energy, so it is natural to want to derive a sense of purpose and fulfillment from our work. In addition, having a sense of purpose at work can bring direction and clarity, leading to greater fulfillment and long-term success—not only professionally but in all areas of life. This feeling of success may fill some of the gaps we are experiencing when we may not feel as fulfilled or confident or worthy in other areas of our lives. Worthiness, redemption, salvation—all hard topics requiring a lot of heart work.

For some, work may provide a sense of identity and self-worth along with financial security and stability. This is because our careers often play a significant role in shaping our daily routines, social interactions, and even our self-concept. Having a job can give individuals a sense of purpose and direction in life. It allows them to feel that they are contributing to society and making a meaningful difference in the world. Additionally, work can provide a sense of accomplishment and pride when individuals are successful in their roles. This feeling of achievement doesn't just boost confidence; it reinforces a person's belief that their efforts matter and contribute to something meaningful, enhancing their overall sense of fulfillment.

Work can also shape how people see themselves and how others see them. For example, someone who identifies as a doctor or an engineer may feel that their profession is an essential part of their identity. They may introduce themselves by stating their profession, and their job title may become a defining characteristic in how others perceive them. While work can provide a sense of purpose and accomplishment, it's important to remember that your worth as a person is not solely defined by your job or your performance at work. People constantly evaluate who they are and where they belong, aiming to better understand themselves and shape their identities. It's natural, then, that some will try to go all in on their workplace and on forming their work identities. However, the more people try to fit into the workplace and suppress their personal identity, the more they begin to adopt the beliefs of those around them—often without even realizing it. Over time, their work identity can start to overshadow their personal values. How do you know if your work identity is starting to take over?

Here's an activity for you to determine how much your work identity shapes your identity overall:

On a scale of one through five, rate yourself on the following.

1= Not At All Like Me   5 = Describes Me Clearly

I have a hard time disconnecting from work: If you find it difficult to switch off from work mode, and constantly check emails or think about work during your off hours, it could be a sign that your work identity is becoming dominant.

1   2   3   4   5

My self-worth is tied to my job: If your sense of self-worth is dependent on your job title, salary, or work achievements, it could indicate that your work identity has taken over your personal identity.

1   2   3   4   5

I neglect my personal life: When you prioritize work over your personal life, such as spending less time with family and friends, pursuing hobbies, or taking care of yourself, it could be a sign that your work identity is becoming all-consuming.

1   2   3   4   5

I feel anxious or stressed when not working: If you feel anxious or stressed when not working, it could be an indication that your work identity has taken over and you have become addicted to the stimulation of work.

1   2   3   4   5

I have lost touch with my values: If your work identity has become dominant, you may lose touch with your personal values, beliefs, and passions that define who you are beyond your job.

1   2   3   4   5

Add up your score here: _____

If your score is between five and ten, then you are in the green zone. Green means that you are at low risk of work or professional identity taking over your entire identity. While you are in the clear, the nervous mother in me wants to tell you to proceed with caution.

If your score was between eleven and seventeen, then you are in the yellow zone. You want to slow down and check yourself. What behaviors are most dominant and potentially toxic to your identity? When people's identities are too tied to their careers, they often struggle to say no at work, which can gradually wear down their sense of self and perspective outside of work.

If your score was between seventeen and twenty-five, then you are in the red zone. My advice is to stop and reevaluate how well this is serving you. What would happen if your company closed tomorrow? Or if you were laid off? Would you feel like you are enough to stand on your own? Are you experiencing sacrificial belonging and potentially mistaking your sacrifices for nobility? Reducing yourself to any single character or defining yourself by a single role—like your job title or performance—can deeply harm your sense of belonging and self-identity.

Experiencing high levels of belonging uncertainty, workplace trauma, and negative behaviors—such as allowing work to take over our lives—can lead to what's known as workplace identity dysmorphia. Workplace identity dysmorphia is the distress and confusion individuals experience when they overly identify with their occupation. In my studies, I've found that the more traumatized and unhealthier participants were, the more they relayed losing their personal identity to take on what was needed to make the company happy. The interplay between personal and social identities and the impact on self-esteem is epic, becoming even more distorted when we introduce workplace trauma.

The Trauma-Informed Workplace

The modern workplace faces an ever-increasing number of challenges as our personal lives and work lives meld into one. People often turn to the workplace to find meaning, purpose, and connection, and companies are quick to position themselves as the destination for belonging. We're in an era of purpose-driven work and workers. Add to that the rising tide of workplace bullying, stress, and anxiety, along with the socio-cultural issues now openly discussed on the job, and it's clear: it's time to change the narrative around workplace trauma and what we are willing to accept. We are at a tipping point where struggling to balance the demands of work and personal life has resulted in heightened levels of "work-life" stress, and it's taking a major toll on employees.

People come into the workplace with implicit values. For some, when they are hired, they try to align their personal values with the company's values. However, once they come into the workplace, they may find themselves facing a series of micro-ethical dilemmas: do I take that personal call during work hours? Do I take extra time for lunch? Do I report my colleague for minor infractions? Do I repeat unfounded rumors on the character and integrity of my colleagues? And still, sometimes they have bigger ethical dilemmas to navigate: do I confront my manager for aggressive or suggestive behavior? Do I challenge policies that threaten the well-being of a local, national, or even global community? In our current political climate, we may find ourselves explicitly defending our political or religious values, and sometimes in behaving in ways that reflect personal values that feel diminished when those values are not aligned with peers, managers, or the corporate landscape. When employees find themselves at a crossroads where their personal values and the company's values clash, generally they are expected to assimilate to company norms, at which point employees may find themselves at a values impasse. Do I sacrifice my mental health and well-being for the job or give up the job for my overall well-being? Can I even afford to do that?

As our personal lives and work lives blend into one, we could argue the two concepts were never really separate. Yet, since the COVID-19 pandemic, these lines seem more blurred. Working to balance the demands of work and personal life has resulted in heightened levels of "work-life" stress, and it's taking a major toll on employees. The constant pressures employees are experiencing have reached a tipping point in the workplace, resulting in trauma in the workplace.

Workplace trauma can come in various forms and can affect employees differently. Here are some examples of workplace trauma:

- **Workplace violence**: Physical assault, verbal abuse, and harassment by coworkers, supervisors, or clients.

- **Discrimination**: Being treated unfairly or experiencing hostility because of race, gender, age, disability, religion, or sexual orientation.

- **Workplace accidents**: Experiencing or witnessing a serious accident, injury, or death at work.

- **Occupational illness**: Developing an illness or injury as a result of work-related activities.

- **Layoffs or job loss**: Losing one's job unexpectedly or being laid off can be traumatic, especially if it is sudden and unexpected.

- **Sexual harassment**: Being subjected to unwanted sexual advances, comments, or behavior by coworkers or supervisors.

- **Workplace bullying**: Repeated, intentional mistreatment by a coworker or supervisor, including verbal abuse, isolation, and humiliation.

- **Work-related PTSD**: Developing post-traumatic stress disorder (PTSD) as a result of experiencing or witnessing a traumatic event at work.

- **High-pressure work environment**: Constantly feeling overwhelmed, stressed, and anxious due to excessive workloads, unrealistic deadlines, or a toxic work environment.

- **Unethical or illegal practices**: Being asked or forced to engage in unethical or illegal practices can be traumatic and can cause long-term emotional and psychological harm.

One of the big problems that we have in the workplace is that we don't share the trauma out loud. It's taboo. It's almost like people believe that those who are successful don't feel pain. Everyone feels pain; it's part of who we are as humans, it helps us grow. We are expected to share the pain in our personal lives, and at times that is applauded, especially for our leaders (you will notice

I use the words *manager* and *leader* interchangeably. I know that they are different words and this will bother some of you, sorry) to share their vulnerability. Yet, when the trauma is caused by the workplace, we are expected to put our masks on and cover ourselves. It's an epic failure in workplace cultures when it could be used for people to band together to do good.

Workplace culture profoundly affects employees' emotional well-being, creating a ripple effect that doesn't stop when we "clock out"—it seeps into our personal lives, impacting our mental health and sense of self. This emotional toll, fueled by workplace-induced trauma, can create the perfect storm, undermining both personal happiness and resilience. Here are some examples:

1. **Bullying**: Workplace bullying can include verbal abuse, harassment, intimidation, and exclusion. Victims of workplace bullying can suffer from anxiety, depression, and post-traumatic stress disorder (PTSD). Bullying can create a toxic work environment where individuals feel uncomfortable and unsafe.

    a. **Verbal abuse:** This includes name-calling, belittling, or shouting at someone, amongst other things. An example of this can be seen through intimidation such as harshly criticizing, insulting, or denouncing another person. It can also be exemplified through micromanagement, as constantly criticizing someone's work or closely monitoring every aspect of their job can be a form of bullying.

    b. **Sabotage:** Deliberately sabotaging someone's work, equipment, or reputation is a form of bullying. This can take the form of starting or spreading false rumors about a colleague, damaging their reputation and relationships with others. Another example is when someone deliberately undermines a colleague's project or idea, making it difficult for them to succeed.

c.   **Gossip:** Gossiping can involve spreading rumors (often untrue) about an individual, causing them to feel embarrassed or ashamed, and inciting feelings of anxiety, depression, and isolation. Gossiping can be used to undermine someone's reputation, making them appear less competent or trustworthy. This can cause the individual to lose respect and trust from their colleagues, leading to feelings of isolation and insecurity. Gossiping can involve sharing personal information about an individual without their consent. This can violate their privacy and cause feelings of embarrassment and shame. Gossiping can also be used to promote negative stereotypes and biases about a particular group or individual. This can lead to discrimination and prejudice in the workplace, causing emotional distress and harm to those affected.

2.   **Gaslighting:** This is when someone manipulates or distorts the truth to make another person doubt their perceptions or reality. Gaslighting in the workplace can be particularly harmful as it can impact an individual's sense of self-worth, confidence, and mental well-being. Here are some examples of gaslighting in the workplace:

a.   **Denying someone's experiences:** An example of this could be when an employee reports experiencing harassment or discrimination, and their employer or coworker denies it ever happened, making the employee question their perception of events.

b.   **Blaming the victim:** In situations where an employee is mistreated, a gaslighter may shift the blame onto the employee, making them feel responsible for the mistreatment and leading them to doubt their self-worth.

c. **Withholding information:** A gaslighter may withhold important information or feedback, making it difficult for an employee to perform their job or improve their performance. This can make the employee feel—and appear—incompetent and question their abilities.

d. **Intimidation:** A gaslighter may use intimidation tactics, such as yelling or threatening behavior, to make an employee feel scared or anxious. Feeling anxious or scared can cause the employee to doubt their judgment and abilities.

e. **Creating confusion:** A gaslighter may deliberately create confusion by providing contradictory information or changing the rules or expectations without notice. This can lead to a feeling of uncertainty and cause an employee to question their judgment and decision-making skills.

3. **Discrimination:** Discrimination can manifest in various ways, including discrimination based on race, gender, age, sexual orientation, religion, and disability. Being the target of discrimination can cause emotional distress, anxiety, and depression.

4. **Unrealistic work expectations:** Being held to unrealistic expectations can lead to burnout and feelings of failure. This can cause emotional distress and feelings of low self-worth.

The list goes on and on.

Psychological Contracts in the Workplace

When companies position themselves as destinations for belonging, they take on the responsibility of fostering it. However, their social and ethical contracts—often called psychological contracts—don't always align with the nuanced reality of belonging, leading to added complexity and confusion. These psychological contracts are the unwritten, implicit expectations and obligations that shape the employee-employer relationship. These expectations are usually set around aspects of job security, career advancement opportunities, work-life balance, compensation and benefits, and the general work environment.

When employees feel that their employer is meeting their expectations and fulfilling their obligations, they are more likely to be engaged and committed to their work. On the other hand, when there is a breach of the psychological contract, it can lead to negative outcomes such as decreased motivation, job dissatisfaction, and turnover.

It's important for employers to be aware of the psychological contracts that exist in their workplace and to manage them effectively. This means being transparent about the expectations and obligations of both parties, regularly communicating with employees, and ensuring that promises made to employees are kept. By doing so, employers can help to build trust and foster positive relationships with their employees, which can lead to a more productive and engaged workforce. While companies have created policies and psychological contracts intending to clarify what is expected of employees, it seems that employees often have different perceptions and experience negative feelings about how well the company executes its commitments.

Initially, policies and psychological contracts were put in place so that employees know what is expected of them and what they can expect from the company, so they are on the same page on the company's mission. However, whether or not the promise has been fulfilled may be open to interpretation, contributing to the feeling of belonging uncertainty and underscoring the importance of understanding how workplaces influence both group and individual senses of belonging. In my research, most participants spoke about unwritten rules in a negative tone. To be fair, it would be shocking if I were to tell you that employees said, "Oh! Oh! Please give me uncertainty and confusion instead of clarity and ease of navigation in the workplace." Here are the top psychological contracts that negatively impact a person's sense of belonging at work as reported by participants.

1. **Unlimited Paid Time Off (PTO)**: Unlimited PTO is a policy that allows employees to take time off work without a set limit on the number of days or hours they can take. While this policy is intended to offer more flexibility and autonomy to employees, most reported that it led them to take little to no time off. Some cited confusion over not knowing how much time to take off, some felt guilty taking time off while their peers were working hard to make up their work. Participants cited that while the company offered unlimited PTO, this was more of a formality and that the culture does not permit the free spirit of taking time off whenever it is needed or wanted. While unlimited PTO may seem like an attractive policy on the surface, it can be confusing and challenging to employees. Companies that choose to adopt this policy should be prepared to provide clear guidelines and communication to their employees and should also be willing to address any issues or concerns that arise as a result of the policy.

2. **Approach HR with caution**: You often hear people say, "HR works for the company, not the employees" and that's 100 percent true. However, that doesn't mean that HR is untrustworthy. There are good people in HR and while most care and want the best for employees, their job is to assess issues through the lens of what makes sense for the company. What's best for the company won't always be what is or seems best for individual employees, which can lead employees to feel HR is "not on their side." Employees have the right to report any incidents of harassment, discrimination, or other workplace issues without fear of retaliation. Retaliation against an employee for making a complaint to HR is illegal and can result in serious consequences for the employer. Yet, participants reported that going to HR may not always be the best option in every situation, citing drawbacks including but not limited to HR not helping resolve their challenges, or HR protecting the interests of the company above employee needs.

3. **Employees should always be on**: Employees need adequate time to rest, recharge, and attend to personal responsibilities outside of work. Employees report feeling like they should always be connected to the company—weekends, weeknights, and PTO be damned. They feel this way for a variety of reasons.

    a. **Technological advancements**: With the increasing use of smartphones, laptops, and other devices, employees can easily stay connected to work even outside of normal work hours. This constant accessibility can make employees feel like they are always on.

    b. **High workload**: When employees have a heavy workload, they may feel pressure to work longer hours or respond to emails and messages outside of work hours. This can lead to a sense of being always on and may contribute to stress and burnout.

c.   **Organizational culture**: Some organizations may have a culture that promotes constant availability and responsiveness. This can create a perception among employees that they are expected to be always on, even if this is not explicitly stated by their employer.

d.   **Personal habits**: Some employees may have personal habits that contribute to feeling always on, such as checking emails or working on projects outside of work hours.

Employees who are constantly "on" face a serious risk of chronic stress, anxiety, and strained relationships. This relentless pressure doesn't just chip away at job satisfaction—it can devastate productivity and lead to a dangerous cycle of burnout and high turnover.

4.   **Always put the company first**: A company will never tell their employees that they need to work 24/7 but they certainly won't stop them from working themselves into the ground to better the company. You can't be loyal to something that can't be loyal back. Loyalty requires reciprocity. If you are loyal to something or someone, you expect that loyalty to be returned in kind. So why are employees putting the company first?

a.   **Job security**: Employees may feel that putting the company's interests first is necessary for their job security. They may believe that being seen as a loyal and dedicated employee will protect their job and ensure their long-term employment.

b.   **Organizational culture**: The culture of an organization can also influence employees to prioritize the company's interests above their own. If the organization promotes a strong sense of loyalty and commitment, employees may feel pressure to align with these values.

c. **Career advancement**: Some employees may feel that putting the company first is necessary for career advancement. They may believe that demonstrating a strong commitment to the company's goals and objectives will help them advance in their care.

d. **Personal values**: For some employees, putting the company first may align with their personal values of hard work, dedication, and loyalty.

Although the goal of organizational social and ethical contracts is a mutual agreement between employee and employer, both sides tend to have different perceptions of how well each side has executed their commitments. In the case of belonging in the workplace, measurement takes place through employee satisfaction and pulse surveys, which do not always show direct links to cause and address belonging issues like the alignment of interpretation. The difference between the employer's definition of belonging in the workplace and the employee's lived experiences and perceptions may not be the same.

What Companies Are Doing to Fix the Trauma Inflicted in the Workplace

The closest that most companies come to addressing workplace trauma is bucketing all common terms and emotions under "work-life stress," throwing those problems over the fence to HR, and calling them belonging issues. It's unfortunate, but these groups do not have a magic wand to wave over stress in the workplace to make it go away. As noted above, the main job of HR is to protect the company. You could argue that protecting employee rights also protects the company from lawsuits, but the reality is that HR needs to focus on the needs and wants of the organization first and foremost. The confusion for most employees is that they want HR to be an advocacy center within the company at large, but while HR organizations aim for advocacy, they also protect the company, and the advocacy and liability aspects are often at odds with one another. In addition, there is a constant stream of problems that HR can't solve because they are not equipped or trained to deal with these constant new challenges. Most companies don't have psychologists on staff and most HR professionals are not trained in dealing with trauma. It's not fair to expect them to.

The constant pressures employees face have reached a breaking point, and with minimal advocacy for individuals, the workplace has become a hotbed of emotional trauma. In the past, the question has been raised: do companies have a responsibility to address said trauma? Underlying this is the larger idea, do companies need to care about their employees' well-being? Let's settle this debate once and for all. **Yes, employers are responsible for the physical and mental well-being of employees**. But why? The surface-level answer is that if you want to attract and retain talent, you should show that you care about employees as individuals. The deeper-level answer is that, by law, employers have a responsibility to provide a safe workplace for employees. Let's start holding them accountable for mental well-being with the same commitment they give to physical safety.

As things stand currently, employees remain in survival mode, navigating rough waters in the workplace without the necessary support from their employers. When employees are in survival mode, it means that they are struggling to meet their basic needs and are constantly in a state of stress or anxiety.

The Age of Fairness in the Workplace

In recent years, companies have expanded their executive boards to include titles with the words *equality* and *diversity* to ensure a more equitable workplace. This reflects a broader movement in society toward greater inclusion and representation of marginalized groups in all aspects of life, including the workplace. Having executives specifically responsible for promoting and ensuring equality and diversity in the workplace can be an effective way for companies to ensure that they are creating an inclusive and equitable environment for all employees. These executives may have a range of responsibilities, including developing and implementing policies to prevent discrimination, promoting diversity in hiring and promotion, and providing training and education to employees on issues related to equity and inclusion.

While the inclusion of these positions on executive boards is a positive step toward greater equality and diversity in the workplace, it's important to note that simply having these positions is not enough. It's also crucial for companies to actively support and empower these executives to make meaningful changes within the organization and to ensure that they are working toward tangible goals and measurable outcomes. Grouping diversity, inclusion, and belonging in these titles implies that each term is interchangeable and synonymous with one another. Yet, the differences between diversity, inclusion, and belonging are not subtle and need to be distinguished better in the workplace to achieve the goals of each. I like to think of them as sisters, not twins—or in this case, triplets.

Belonging is not diversity and it's not inclusion. While diversity, inclusion, and belonging have different meanings, they are often grouped together to encourage fairness, with belonging being the endgame. Sometimes equality and equity are thrown in for good measure. It always surprises me when I read an article or a book with the title of diversity, inclusion, and belonging in it and belonging is barely mentioned or referred to as an afterthought, but here we are. I dare you, look up any workplace diversity, inclusion, and belonging report—are there any belonging metrics in here? You won't find them. Lumping diversity, inclusion, and belonging together is doing them a disservice respectively, so let's separate them to stand tall, each on their own.

Diversity refers to the presence of individuals from different backgrounds, cultures, and identities in the workplace. It is important for organizations to recognize and value diversity, as it can bring different perspectives, skills, and experiences to the table. Diverse representation does not automatically form an inclusive workplace, and high-performing companies realize that to achieve both diversity and inclusion, they need to embrace and accommodate different styles of thinking.

Simply having a diverse workforce is not enough. It is also important to create an inclusive environment where everyone feels welcomed and valued. Inclusion refers to creating a workplace culture where everyone feels respected, valued, and supported, regardless of their background or identity. This means creating policies, practices, and systems that enable all employees to fully participate and contribute to the organization. Inclusive workplaces value and leverage all employees' unique perspectives and experiences, which can lead to increased innovation, creativity, and productivity.

Of the terms used most interchangeably, inclusion and belonging in the workplace are most easily confused. Both symbolize connection and acceptance, but cognitively they are different. While others determine inclusion, belonging is something that we negotiate with ourselves. That's right—you are the only one who can truly determine whether you feel belonging or not. Everything external is inclusion or exclusion.

The Link between Psychological Safety and Belonging

Psychological safety has become synonymous with fairer treatment in the workplace. This stems from the notion that in times of change, depression, stress, and fear, companies should create the psychological safety that employees need. The reality is that psychological safety should be table stakes. Psychological safety refers to the sense of confidence and trust that employees have in expressing their thoughts, ideas, and concerns without fear of negative consequences such as ridicule, rejection, or punishment. This concept is particularly important in addressing workplace trauma because it creates an environment in which individuals feel comfortable sharing their experiences and seeking support.

While feeling psychologically safe makes team members and individuals feel accepted and respected, it does not guarantee a sense of belonging but it helps. When one feels psychologically unsafe, it is difficult to feel a sense of belonging. Employees reported that when they feel psychological safety in the workplace, especially from their managers and leaders, this increases their sense of belonging. For example, in talking with an employee about a rough situation she was handling in the workplace, she told me, "We had a rough conversation, but I felt safe enough in that moment to be able to say something and align the way that we operate. I'm really thankful that she created the psychological safety for me to be able to have that conversation with her. To me, you need to feel psychologically safe in order to feel like you belong with your manager. That's what connects us." Interestingly, it can also be a "chicken and the egg" thing. Employees say that when they experience belonging, they also feel a degree of safety at work in being able to express their ideas and thoughts and exist without fear of consequences, to be themselves.

Conversely, when employees don't feel psychologically safe, it leads to thwarted belonging. One employee told me they stayed with the company, despite not feeling safe, because she didn't know what else to do. The employee felt stuck and she told me, "I guess it's years of Stockholm syndrome. I know the way that I am treated is not right and I don't feel like I can speak up. At this point, I don't know what's normal and not normal. I only know that I will get yelled out for stepping out of line. It weighs on me, heavily." Even worse, this feeling can last long after the employee has left that job and that workplace. Participants reported that they were unable to feel psychologically safe even in new jobs and environments because they had not dealt with PTSD from prior manager gaslighting, toxicity, and torment that continued to plague them in response to trauma.

Through the lens of psychological safety, companies have an opportunity to reduce confusion and mental anguish and increase true belonging in the workplace. To promote psychological safety related to belonging in the workplace, employers can take several steps:

1. **Foster an open and inclusive culture**: Establishing an environment where employees feel respected and valued, inclusive of their background or experiences, can help build trust and a sense of belonging.

2. **Encourage open communication**: Provide opportunities for employees to share their thoughts and ideas openly, such as through regular team meetings and feedback channels.

3. **Provide resources for support**: Offer counseling services or resources for employees who may be struggling with the effects of workplace trauma (both past and present).

4. **Teach leaders how to lead**: There is an assumption that needs to be squashed, that leaders automatically know how to lead. Leaders are not born knowing how to lead; they are made and transformed through lived experiences. Of course, some have natural leadership skills and talents, but we can't assume that's the case for everyone, and even talented people can and should improve their leadership skills.

5. **Model positive behaviors**: Leaders can model behaviors that demonstrate the importance of psychological safety, such as actively listening, being responsive, and showing empathy.

6. **Take action**: If an employee reports an incident of workplace trauma, it's essential to take appropriate action promptly. This shows that the organization takes these issues seriously and prioritizes the well-being of its employees.

By prioritizing psychological safety, employers can help prevent workplace trauma and support employees struggling with its effects.

Chapter 3

Workplace Bravery, and All the Stuff

Rings are bright and shiny and pretty—and precious. None more precious than the One Ring in *The Lord of the Rings* trilogy.[15] Our hero, Frodo Baggins, is entrusted with the task of destroying the ring. Despite the immense weight of this responsibility, Frodo accepts the challenge and sets out on a perilous journey across Middle-earth, ultimately showing us that while we think of bravery as doing something without being scared, bravery is about moving ahead despite our fears. Here's the thing about bravery: if you are doing it right, it can feel like fear. When someone exhibits bravery, they are often putting themselves in a vulnerable position and taking a risk, especially in the workplace.

One thing I'm great at is burying the lede. You may be thinking, "Hello...the book is called *Braving the Workplace*—and it took her until Chapter 3 to get there. Oy vey!" Starting with bravery would have been like throwing you in the deep end of the pool before you had your first swim lesson and I'm not the sink-or-swim type of gal, so I wanted to give you floaties first. Belonging, the history of work, and workplace trauma are all complex, but they give you the boost you need to get into bravery. And now I'm stalling, and why? Bravery in the workplace is, well, tough. The good news, though: you've survived 100 percent of your worst days.

What Is Bravery in the Workplace?

Bravery in the workplace refers to the willingness of employees to take bold and courageous actions to achieve positive outcomes, even in the face of uncertainty or risk. It involves stepping outside of your comfort zone and challenging yourself to confront difficult or uncomfortable situations. That's the general, politically correct answer but when I did the research, I got several different answers. All names are anonymous (to protect the innocent).

- **Workplace bravery is** "taking action when you see, hear, observe or experience inappropriate behavior toward you or others. Your action doesn't have to be loud or attention seeking. It could simply be asking a clarifying question, addressing a microaggression, or making sure you include someone that is not being included. It's about displaying the right behaviors for the right reasons." Thank you, A.

- **Workplace bravery is** "remaining silent. I must be silent because although the workplace asks me to be vulnerable, they aren't equipped to handle my truth. It's when you are afraid and doing it anyway. I still need to wear a mask in a place that asks me to be myself or I will be out of a job. So, bravery is showing up, trying to make a dent with inequities where I can, and supporting my family by putting up with ignorance on a daily basis." Thank you, B.

- **Workplace bravery is** "standing up against the system that doesn't want to change and pointing out where and how that same system can be modified to work for everyone. It's about speaking truth to power and holding them accountable for making changes that you help them uncover from employee data and lived experiences. It's also about telling the truth when bad actors with great influence have more political savvy than you do." Thank you, J.

- **Workplace bravery is** "staring directly into the face of workplace gaslighting and staying with a company despite bad leadership to work on the system and help your coworkers survive. It requires an individual to stand up for their own mental well-being and values, even when it means going against the grain or risking their job security." Thank you, B.

- **Workplace bravery is** "approaching a tough situation with a mindset of *get curious, not furious*. Go into that moment to seek understanding rather than being accusatory. Seek understanding, share my perspective, and ask, 'but how do you see it?' Share 'this is how I see it' and then really listen when you ask questions. This approach requires you to lean into your vulnerability." Thank you, D.

How does workplace bravery show up? What are some examples that help bring it home?

- An example of workplace bravery is...**speaking up against unethical practices**: A brave employee might raise concerns about unethical behavior, even if it means risking their reputation or facing potential backlash from colleagues or superiors.

- An example of workplace bravery is...**challenging the status quo**: A brave individual might propose innovative ideas that challenge established norms or processes, even if it involves stepping into uncharted territory and facing resistance from others.

- An example of workplace bravery is...**advocating for marginalized groups**: A brave employee might stand up for the rights and fair treatment of marginalized colleagues, addressing issues such as discrimination, inequality, or lack of diversity.

So, I've concluded bravery in the workplace is being yourself, despite the sensation of sacrificing who you are to fit in. Bravery in the workplace is embracing who you are and what you stand for as a superpower. Bravery in the workplace is often swimming through treacherous waters and not letting the bastards get you down, because damn, they will try. Bravery in the workplace is navigating cultural norms and in-the-box thinking telling you to be yourself and then reprimanding you for doing it—it is holding your head high and belonging to yourself.

Sacrifice

Bravery seems to be a contradictory concept. Some felt strongly that it comes from a positive place of empowerment, morality, and noble sacrifice, while others described it as coming from negative emotions like fear, bullying, shame, and suffering-based sacrifice. Yes, I have sacrificed there twice. It's so damn complex. Yes, sacrifice can be a part of bravery. In many cases, being brave involves putting oneself at risk or making personal sacrifices for the benefit of others or for a greater cause. For example, a soldier putting their life on the line to protect their country, a firefighter rushing into a burning building to save lives, or a healthcare worker risking their own health to care for patients during a pandemic are all examples of bravery that involve noble sacrifice.

Sacrifice can take many forms, including giving up personal time, resources, comfort, or even safety. It often requires a willingness to put the needs of others or a cause above one's own needs or desires. While sacrifice can be difficult and sometimes painful, it can also be a powerful expression of bravery and a way to make a positive impact on the world. The question is, when does sacrifice go from noble and supportive to self-sacrificing and destructive? Sacrifice starts to become dangerous when it involves risking one's physical or mental well-being to an extreme or unhealthy extent. Here are a few situations where sacrifice can become dangerous in the workplace:

- **Physical health**: Sacrificing one's physical health by consistently working long hours without proper rest or neglecting self-care can lead to burnout, exhaustion, and physical ailments. Ignoring signs of fatigue, not taking breaks, or consistently pushing beyond healthy limits can have detrimental effects on one's well-being.

- **Mental health**: Sacrificing one's mental health by constantly subjecting oneself to high levels of stress, anxiety, or emotional strain without seeking support or taking care of one's mental well-being can lead to mental health issues. Ignoring the signs of stress, not addressing emotional needs, or consistently enduring toxic work environments can be harmful in the long run.

- **Relationships and personal life**: Sacrificing personal relationships, family time, or personal interests excessively for work-related commitments can strain relationships and lead to a sense of isolation or disconnection. Neglecting personal life for extended periods can lead to feelings of regret, loneliness, and imbalance.

- **Boundaries**: Sacrificing personal boundaries by consistently saying yes to additional work or responsibilities without considering one's own capacity or limits can result in overwhelming stress and an inability to manage workload effectively. Ignoring personal boundaries can lead to a lack of work-life balance and contribute to a sense of being constantly overwhelmed.

- **Belonging**: If you are sacrificing who you are, what makes you, you, you are in dangerous territory. While self-sacrifice can be seen as unselfishly giving over oneself or one's own interest for others, it can also lead to sacrificing parts of your identity including your values, beliefs, and principles.

But why does workplace bravery require sacrifice and is it worth it if it can be so dangerous? The short answer is workplace bravery often requires sacrifice because it involves taking risks and challenging the status quo, which can come with personal costs or trade-offs. If people know it's wrong or unsafe, why are they still doing it?

Is it worth it? Yes, if it is not dangerous to you—and a clear way to identify the boundary line is assessing whether or how much you're experiencing any of the above, as compared to positive effects contributing to your growth like the following:

- **Stepping outside of the comfort zone**: Workplace bravery often entails pushing beyond one's comfort zone and embracing new challenges or unfamiliar situations. This may require sacrificing the comfort and familiarity of existing roles or routines, and taking on new responsibilities or projects that demand additional effort, time, or skill development.

- **Risking reputation or status quo**: Bravery in the workplace can involve challenging the status quo, questioning established practices, or proposing innovative ideas. This may entail sacrificing one's reputation or acceptance by others who may be resistant to change or critical of unconventional approaches in the name of doing the right thing, doing good.

- **Speaking up against injustice**: Bravery can manifest in speaking up against unfairness, inequality, or unethical behavior in the workplace. This may require sacrificing one's silence or conformity, and potentially facing backlash, reprisals, or social consequences for confronting those in positions of power—also for doing what's right, doing good.

- **Making tough decisions**: Bravery often involves making difficult decisions that may have significant consequences. This may require sacrificing personal comfort, popularity, or short-term benefits to make choices that align with long-term goals, values, or the best interests of the organization, stakeholders, and a team.

It's all about striking a balance and ensuring that the sacrifices made are reasonable and responsible and do not disproportionately harm an individual's well-being. Organizations can foster a supportive environment that acknowledges and rewards acts of bravery—specifically those that "get it done and do it right"—without the danger. There is a call to action here: companies, stop praising dangerous behaviors that contribute to a toxic culture in the name of bravery and courage in the workplace.

Courage and Bravery— Another Set of Sisters, Not Twins

Speaking of courage, *courage* and *bravery* are often used interchangeably, but there are subtle differences between the two. The word *courage* comes from the French root *cour* or *coeur*, which means heart. In today's workplace, courage generally refers to the ability to face difficult or challenging situations with confidence and determination, even in the face of fear or uncertainty.

It involves the willingness to take risks or make sacrifices in pursuit of a goal and may involve facing physical danger or emotional hardship.

On the other hand, the root of the word *brave* can be traced back to both the Old Italian and Old Spanish word *bravo*. Both originally meant "bold" or "fierce." The word *bravo* further derives from the Latin word "barbarus," meaning "barbarian" or "foreigner." Over time, the meaning of *bravo* evolved to connote courage, valor, and fearlessness, which are the qualities associated with being brave today. Bravery typically refers specifically to the willingness to confront and overcome fear in the face of danger or adversity. It assumes that taking action will occur and be motivated in the face of fear, such as running into a burning building to save someone or standing up to a bully. When we talk about someone brave, you'll often hear that they have a lot of heart. Ironic, huh, since the root and true meaning of courage is heart—again, making them sisters, not twins.

In general, courage is a more general concept that can apply to a wide range of situations, while bravery is more specific to situations that involve danger or physical risk. However, the two concepts are closely related and often overlap in practice, particularly in the context of the workplace. Courage in the workplace often involves challenging the status quo, voicing dissenting opinions, or taking responsibility for one's actions and decisions. Bravery in the workplace can be displayed by individuals who willingly put themselves at risk or make personal sacrifices to achieve positive outcomes or protect others.

What are some tangible examples of workplace courage?

- Workplace courage can look like...**sharing constructive feedback**: A courageous employee may provide honest and

constructive feedback to colleagues or superiors, even if it
is uncomfortable or might provoke initial resistance.

- Workplace courage can look like...**taking calculated risks**:
A courageous individual might propose a new initiative or
strategy, acknowledging the potential risks involved but
believing in the potential positive outcomes and taking
measured steps to mitigate those risks.

- Workplace courage can look like...**admitting mistakes and
taking responsibility**: A courageous employee may openly
acknowledge their mistakes, take responsibility for them,
and work toward rectifying the situation, even if it means
facing potential consequences or accountability.

- Workplace courage can look like...**embracing change**:
A courageous employee might proactively embrace
organizational change, adapt to new technologies or
processes, and support others in navigating the transitions,
even if it involves leaving their comfort zone.

While courage and bravery share similarities and often go
hand in hand, courage emphasizes the internal strength and
determination to act despite fear, while bravery inspires to
conquer fear. Both courage and bravery in the workplace enable
individuals to navigate challenges, drive positive change, and
make a difference in their organizations and teams.

The Link between Vulnerability and Workplace Bravery (and Courage)

Every company is talking about vulnerability—it's all the rage.
You hear them all say, "You can bring your authentic selves to

work as long as you are vulnerable and courageous and brave."
But is that true? There is always some level of risk. But when is it
worth the risk?

Before we go any further, *vulnerability* refers to the willingness to
be open, authentic, and emotionally exposed, even in the face of
uncertainty or potential rejection. Workplace courage and bravery
often involve taking emotional risks, such as sharing innovative
ideas, challenging the status quo, or engaging in difficult
conversations. These actions require individuals to be vulnerable
by expressing their thoughts and opinions, knowing that they may
face criticism, disagreement, or rejection. However, they need a
safe space to do it as vulnerability and workplace courage and
bravery are closely tied to psychological safety. When employees
feel psychologically safe, they are more likely to be vulnerable and
demonstrate courage and bravery by speaking up and taking risks.

The problem is employees see smoke and mirrors—companies say
to be vulnerable, but some employees feel like that vulnerability
may be used against them. It is much easier for leaders to
compartmentalize their employees—this is work Beth vs. Beth "at
home." It's easier for the leaders to stick to the "work Beth" and
think they should keep it strictly business instead of learning more
about Beth as a person overall, complexities included. Maybe there
is a fear of "if I get to know Beth then I have to care about her; if I
know her son is in cancer remission, I take the risk of having to ask
her about it when I talk to her next."

Workplace culture tells us that we need to embrace vulnerability
to take bold actions or express our ideas and opinions. In searching
the internet, here is how vulnerability and workplace courage are
connected through corporate speak:

- Vulnerability fosters...**authenticity**, as individuals willing
  to be vulnerable are more likely to show their true selves
  and share their genuine thoughts and feelings. Workplace

courage thrives in environments where authenticity is valued and trusted, as it encourages individuals to take risks and express their ideas without fear of judgment or negative consequences.

- Vulnerability creates...**opportunities for connection and collaboration** within the workplace. When individuals are willing to be vulnerable and share their perspectives, experiences, and challenges, it fosters a sense of empathy and understanding among team members. This, in turn, encourages collaboration, innovative thinking, and collective problem-solving, all of which require workplace courage.

- Vulnerability contributes to...**personal and professional growth**. By embracing vulnerability and taking courageous actions, individuals open themselves to new experiences, feedback, and learning opportunities. They are more likely to challenge themselves, step outside their comfort zones, and pursue continuous improvement.

These are great, all of them...but only when companies' words match their actions. I would go as far as to say that most employees want to be their authentic selves and appropriately vulnerable but taking off the mask and the armor that keeps them alive, employed, is too big a risk for them to take. In my case, I took off the mask to my then-manager about my son's cancer and later, feeling suicidal and what happened? *Nothing*— that jerk said *nothing*, twice. First about cancer and then suicide. You may be thinking, *that's one dude and he was inconsiderate* (understatement), but my story is not limited to me. Many of us wear masks and some of us wear full body armor. I took the mask off out of desperation. *Nothing*. Believe it or not, *nothing* taught me that my vulnerability is a strength and the shame associated with this interaction with my manager was not a reflection of me, that's all him.

You can only control what you put out there, not other people. It was not safe for me to take my mask off and maybe you could argue that I should have learned my lesson when I spoke to him about my son's cancer. I wanted, so badly, to be liked by him, to be cared about. So, while it was not safe to take off my mask—and I did it anyway—it was a win. Yes, I said *win*. Did it feel like a win at the time? No freaking way. It taught me that some things break our hearts but fix our vision—vulnerability did that for me. The second that *nothing* happened the second time, I was done. He gave me no reasons to believe, no reasons to stay. *Nothing* was my tipping point to leave. It was the push I needed to quit and take myself out of harm's way. Since then, the risk and emotional exposure have been way less scary to me and dare I say it, while vulnerability is high risk, it's even higher reward (and it can do the same thing for you).

When Is It Safe to Be Vulnerable at Work?

I'm a huge Bob Dylan fan, and in a 1977 conversation with Jonathan Cott, he said, "You must be vulnerable to be sensitive to reality. And to me being vulnerable is just another way of saying that one has nothing more to lose."[16] While I believe his words, I can't help but think, *do his words reflect the reality of the modern worker?* I mean, what does Bob Dylan have to lose? He is a legend, an icon. He can say whatever he wants, and no one is going to fire him. He isn't living paycheck to paycheck or even dependent on his music at this point to secure his livelihood as he may have done in 1977. Yet, what he is saying is not lip service; it's meant to be inspirational. And truly, he was vulnerable and brave way before it was cool. He wore his vulnerability like a badge of honor and inspired a generation to speak up and be brave.

It's such an oxymoron: all of our lives we are taught by parents, teachers, community members, and heroes like Bob Dylan to be brave, but then we get to the workplace, and we try to play it safe. So, when is it safe to be vulnerable, to take the mask off and believe that our vulnerability won't be weaponized? I want to give you sage advice, but you need to pay attention to the attitudes, behaviors, and responses of leaders and colleagues to gauge the level of psychological safety and support for vulnerability. Vulnerability is not comfortable, so if you are waiting to be vulnerable when it's comfy cozy, that's not how it works. The good news is, we grow when we are uncomfortable—and if you learn to lean into that discomfort, you too will grow. Here are the things you should ask yourself when looking to be more vulnerable at work:

1. **Will your conditions be met?** You have standards and you don't want to lower your bar to meet someone else's. Settling will make you feel bad, and sacrificing who you are will make you feel even worse. Before opening up and using the power of vulnerability, make sure it's for something meaningful. Is it a hill worth dying on? If it is for your integrity and your values, the answer is yes.

2. **Is there mutual trust?** When there is mutual trust, individuals can open up and be vulnerable, knowing that their vulnerabilities will be respected, heard, and met with empathy and support.

3. **Do your leaders model vulnerability?** When leaders model vulnerability, encourage open communication, and respond to vulnerability with empathy and understanding, it creates a culture where others feel safe to be vulnerable.

4. **Does the culture value and respect diversity and inclusivity?** A workplace culture that values diversity, inclusivity, and respect provides a foundation for safety in vulnerability.

When individuals feel accepted and valued for their unique experiences and perspectives, they are more likely to feel safe sharing their vulnerabilities.

5. **Does the culture embrace mistakes and failure?** When these are viewed as opportunities for growth, individuals feel safer sharing their vulnerabilities, knowing that they contribute to individual and organizational learning.

6. **Do you feel belonging uncertainty?** If you are going through a lot of uneasiness and feel like this may not be the place for you, it's especially hard to know if it's a good time to be vulnerable at work. By now, if you are experiencing belonging uncertainty, the aligned question may also be, **Do you have a backup plan?** Speaking up when you are feeling belonging uncertainty is key; it's vulnerability and protection of your mental health and if you have a safe space as your safety net or a new beginning, then why not speak up for yourself?

Organizations have a unique opportunity in front of them, recognizing the link between vulnerability and workplace courage, and moving from lip service to action. They can create an environment that encourages individuals to be authentic, take risks, and express their ideas openly. Take a leader's first approach by training your leaders on modeling vulnerability in practice and making it safe.

It's sad but true, but we still see many leaders perceive vulnerability as an awkward liability. It's true—leaders worry that leading with vulnerability or even expressing it at all negatively impacts how they are seen as an authority figure in the organization. Those leaders are the ones typically worried about managing up, monkey see monkey do. Senior executive leaders need to make vulnerability safe because when done right, their downline leaders establish trust earlier on and throughout their relationships with subordinates. Leaders: leading with vulnerability shows your people who you are beyond your title, beyond the numbers, and beyond the corporate speak they hear day in and day out. Show them who you are as a person—it starts with you. Change the narrative and behaviors and you will change the experience to foster a true sense of belonging using vulnerability as a strength.

Maybe Bob Dylan had it right, but instead of looking at things in the current reality, maybe what you need is to change your reality, the perceptions that shape your reality, and your bravery in the workplace.

Bravery and Resilience

Who remembers Young's Modulus, also known as the Modulus of Elasticity from high school physics? Young's Modulus is a measure of a material's stiffness or ability to resist deformation when subjected to external forces. It quantifies the relationship between stress (force per unit area) and strain (resulting deformation) in a material. Modulus of elasticity reflects a material's ability to withstand stress and strain *without permanent deformation*. It's a principle that basically says every object has the ability to bend until it breaks. When I think of corporate resilience and bravery in the workplace, I think of Young's Modulus...another case of sisters, not twins.

Corporate resilience refers to an organization's ability to adapt, recover, and thrive in the face of various challenges, such as economic downturns, market volatility, technological disruptions, or natural disasters. I would like one thing added, similar to Young's Modulus: *without permanent deformation*. Corporate resilience encompasses factors such as strategic planning, risk management, operational flexibility, financial stability, and the ability to withstand and respond to unexpected events. While Young's Modulus is primarily a property of materials, not corporations, we can draw some metaphorical analogies between the two concepts to illustrate their relationship. Leaders are putting the onus onto their employees similar to Young's Modulus, stress-testing them—but the interesting part is, they don't think about what happens when they break. There are a million and one reasons why this happens. Sometimes it's because leaders are not connected to their employees; sometimes they don't realize how much influence they have. One thing is certain: all materials can break over time, and humans are no exception.

Picture this: layoffs happen. All the corporate phrases you can handle (and then some) come out of the woodwork:

> "We need you to do more with less."

> "Even though we let go of half of our staff, the work needs to get done somehow, and you need to make it happen."

> "Sorry, we can't offer you a raise for taking on more; stay strong."

> "Suck it up, it won't be forever."

Sound familiar? I'm sure you've heard it all before. Each one is extremely triggering to employees. When employers promote resilience as a fix for employee concerns without addressing the root causes of dissatisfaction, it only adds to employee stress and distress—pushing them to their breaking point. When resilience is a forced response to distress, employers must confront their responsibility in creating the sources of distress when resilience is imposed as a compulsory reaction. For example, my friend Pim's company has small-scale layoffs every year, like clockwork. After each round is complete, Pim's company hosts what they call Survivor Week. It's part "Yay, you made it, let's celebrate" and part "Now that the dust is settling, how will all of you survivors now pick up the pieces?" So many things are wrong with this; the name alone could be talked about for ten pages. What happens during Survivor Week? There are a lot of planning meetings, reallocation of work, and more happy hours than you can shake a stick at so people can regroup and recalibrate.

Pim said employees dread Survivor Week. It feels wrong; they are still processing the layoffs the week before, and it is mentally and physically exhausting—long hours and no acknowledgment of the underlying issues that got them to this place. She said she's tired of bearing the burden of leadership's poor choices. A few years ago, employees even joined forces to tell leadership that "Survivor Week" is nearly as toxic as the layoff week that precedes it. The reaction? Leadership blasted their employees saying Survivor Week is a way to celebrate and that they should be grateful that they still have jobs. Pim's company twisted the situation, leaving the remaining employees feeling blamed and manipulated—as if they were being disrespectful. The company exploited its employees' ability to bounce back from adversity or cope with a difficult situation. They could have used this as an opportunity to listen to their employees and help them adapt, recover, and maintain psychological well-being in the face of stress, but they did not, and while not all companies have Survivor Week, they experience similar distress.

This is called weaponizing resiliency and it occurs when individuals are blamed for systems in place, wrongdoings, and shortfalls of the companies. Employers put the burden on their employees, urging them to be resilient when things go wrong at work rather than taking accountability, prioritizing self-care, and fostering a healthy work-life balance. Employers are putting the burden on the employee instead of recognizing the importance of personal well-being, and it is causing workplace trauma—which is ironic since trauma and poor decisions are usually why companies are asking for "resilience" in the first place. They are essentially praising individuals for their perseverance or grit through said trauma, without considering the need for a sustainable and balanced approach to work and life. For individuals, this feels good in the short term, to push through and make a situation like this work, but like Young's Modulus, it's only a matter of time until they break. Organizations should resist the temptation to rely solely on their employees' resilience and instead recognize the need to address the underlying systems and structures within their organization that contribute to the difficulty of being resilient.

Don't get me wrong—resilience is a wonderful and necessary skill. Resilience is the continued pursuit of goals despite adversity, and it builds strength in epic ways. You need to be mindful of how companies position it. There is a strong link between bravery and resilience, and you want to make sure it's on your terms. Both bravery and resilience involve facing challenges, adversity, and setbacks. Resilience can be valuable in overcoming challenges, but it does not possess a magical ability to automatically resolve underlying concerns, issues, or pain—and it's not an infinite resource. When managers observe that their teams are on the verge of collapse due to burnout, their immediate focus should be on addressing the root causes of that burnout rather than enrolling their employees in questionable grit-building training programs or asking employees to get it done at all costs. The cost of that kind of ask is potentially limitless. You land yourself in the sacrificial and potentially thwarted belonging zone.

Bravery and Success

While success can be defined in various ways depending on individual goals and circumstances, bravery can significantly contribute to achieving success. Bravery involves taking risks, facing challenges, and stepping outside of one's comfort zone. These qualities are often necessary for achieving success, as success often requires taking bold action and making difficult decisions. For example, successful entrepreneurs often need to take risks and make bold decisions to build and grow their businesses; successful athletes need to push themselves beyond their limits and take risks to achieve victory; successful leaders need to make tough decisions and take responsibility for the outcomes, even in the face of uncertainty and risk.

Bravery alone is not enough to achieve success. Success often requires a combination of bravery, hard work, persistence, and sometimes even luck. Additionally, it's important to balance bravery with careful consideration and strategic thinking to minimize risks and maximize the chances of success. Bravery involves recognizing and seizing opportunities when they arise. Success is often a result of being proactive, identifying potential opportunities, and having the courage to pursue them. Bravery allows individuals to capitalize on favorable situations, whether it's starting a new venture, pursuing a promotion, or initiating a challenging project. Bravery is essential for navigating obstacles and setbacks on the path to success. Success rarely comes without encountering challenges and failures along the way.

Success

Success in life looks different for each person because everyone has unique goals, values, and life experiences that shape their perspective on what they consider to be successful. For example, one person may define success as achieving financial stability and material wealth, while another person may prioritize personal relationships and emotional fulfillment as their definition of success. Additionally, cultural and societal norms can influence how success is defined within a particular community or group. Each person's journey toward success is also unique, with varying challenges, opportunities, and resources available to them.

The workplace is no different, or is it? Success in the workplace can look different depending on the specific industry, job, and individual goals. Traditionally, some common indicators of workplace success may include:

1. **Positive impact on the company:** Success in the workplace can be measured by the positive impact an individual or team has on the company's overall success. This could be through increased revenue, cost savings, or improving overall performance.

2. **Job satisfaction:** Feeling fulfilled and satisfied in one's job can be a sign of success. This could include having a positive work-life balance, feeling valued and appreciated by colleagues and supervisors, and finding personal fulfillment in the work being done.

3. **Recognition and advancement:** Advancement within a company or industry can be a sign of success. This could be in the form of a promotion, salary increase, or being recognized as an expert or leader in the field.

4. **Achieving goals and targets:** Success in the workplace often involves meeting or exceeding specific goals and targets set by the employer or individual employee. This could be in the form of sales targets, project deadlines, income level, or other measurable objectives.

Defining success for yourself brings clarity to your goals and helps you build a roadmap to reach them.

What Does Success Look Like for You?

_____

_____

_____

Are you there now? Yes or No

If no, why not?

_____

_____

_____

I'm curious, did you write about work in your definition of success? Did you include other expectations as well? Is career success sufficient alone or do you expect more of yourself regarding success?

Did you include notions of balance, recognition, contributing, having freedom, or wealth? Was there a high importance placed on relationships?

I'm guessing you may have edited your answers after I fired off questions and asked you to add specific goals in terms of success criteria, maybe with details not pertaining to the job. Go back as many times as you like.

Success in the Workplace

In the workplace, success is often measured by straightforward metrics: hitting business goals, meeting performance targets, driving revenue or profit, finishing projects and reports on time— much like the endless, questionable TPS reports in *Office Space*.[17] These outcomes are typically quantifiable and tangible, used to evaluate an employee's performance and contributions to the organization. The pressure to meet performance targets, deliver results, and meet deadlines can create a high-stress environment that can be challenging to navigate. Several factors can contribute to this stress:

1. **High expectations**: When employees are expected to achieve high levels of performance consistently, it can create pressure to maintain that level of performance and deliver results.

2. **Tight deadlines**: When deadlines are tight, or there are multiple competing priorities, employees may feel like they don't have enough time to complete their work, leading to increased stress and anxiety.

3. **Fear of failure**: Employees may feel pressure to succeed because they fear the consequences of failure, such

as negative feedback, reduced job security, or missed opportunities for career advancement.

4. **Perceived lack of control**: When employees feel like they have little control over their work environment or the outcomes of their work, it can create a sense of helplessness and increase stress levels.

5. **Competition with colleagues**: Competition with colleagues for recognition, rewards, or promotions can create a stressful and high-pressure environment.

6. **Belonging uncertainty**: Belonging uncertainty can cause stress because it creates a sense of ambiguity and unpredictability in an individual's social environment. When individuals are uncertain about their place on a team, in the company, with peers, or with their manager, it can lead to insecurity, anxiety, and stress.

So, it's great to have measurable goals and want to achieve success, but any of the factors that contribute to a stressful environment in 1–6 above can interfere and suck. They feel so bad. So, how can you avoid the suck?

1. **Make success multi-threaded**: When workplace success is seen as the ultimate life goal, the ultimate success, individuals can feel disconnected from their family and peers, regardless of whether they fail or succeed. If you are succeeding at work and reach your desired goal, it is common that your mind will move the target, so work may feel like an endless pursuit which may lead to burnout, and you will need a different outlet to relieve stress. This might surprise the workaholics, but a life outside of work helps you become more successful and productive in your professional life. If you fail at work when you have no outlets, you feel like a total failure—that can become dangerous and

       lead to a thwarted sense of belonging which puts you in a painful mental state.

2. **Make success about more than outcomes**: Success at work can also be about the processes and behaviors that lead to those outcomes. It involves a combination of skills, behaviors, relationships, and contributions that lead to individual and organizational growth and success. For example, an employee who consistently demonstrates teamwork, collaboration, and innovation may be considered successful even if they haven't directly contributed to a specific outcome. In addition, success in the workplace can also be measured by personal and professional growth, learning new skills, building relationships, and making a positive impact on the organization and its stakeholders.

3. **Think of your job as a verb rather than a noun**: Get out of the habit of describing yourself as your job. For example, instead of saying, "Hi, I'm Beth and I'm a belonging researcher," I could swap that out with, "Hi, I'm Beth and I do belonging research." You are more than an occupation. You are more than achieved numbers, you are more than productivity, and you are more than an employee. Embrace the whole you. Remember, when it comes to this chapter and the next, you are the author. Take control of the narrative, your identity. When your identity is based on your job, it is no longer within your control, and you are giving that control to your job. You are more, so much more than your job...so make sure not to put all of your eggs in the workplace basket.

While we don't want companies dictating their employees' narrative, we do want them to help their employees play the long game, protecting their employees' mental health and inspiring them to thrive. At the same time, companies can improve their retention by helping employees define success beyond their bottom-line profits. In fact, helping employees measure success should have a myriad of factors. Here are some of the factors that companies should encourage and measure with their employees to strike a better, braver balance in the workplace:

1. **Goal-setting**: Employers should encourage employees to set specific, measurable, achievable, relevant, and time-bound (SMART) goals that align with the company's overall objectives. While goals of this type don't fulfill all definitions of success, setting goals can help employees stay focused, motivated, and accountable and can help ensure that their efforts are aligned with the company's strategic priorities. Setting goals around productivity, utilization, and attainment is where the bottom-line numbers can come into play.

2. **Continuous learning**: Employers should encourage employees to engage in ongoing learning and professional development. Employees should also arrange the conditions to make it more likely that the employees will engage with these opportunities. This can include attending conferences and workshops, taking courses, pursuing certifications, or participating in mentorship programs. By investing in their learning and development, employees can enhance their skills, knowledge, and expertise, and contribute more effectively to the company's success. This also gives employees the opportunity to recharge and refresh.

3. **See your employees as their whole selves:** Employers should encourage leaders to foster and collaborate with their employees in a whole new way, based on the employee's personal values and goals. Learn who they are outside of the workplace and how it impacts how they show up in the workplace. Employees want to succeed in a way that enriches their lives both in and out of the workplace. Look at your employees as members of their own units, for example, within their families (not to be confused with workplace

familism, which we will discuss soon). The unit being the person and their family, their interests, their aspirations, what gives them meaning, etc. Factoring in details about your employees will help you both generate new ideas, solve problems differently, and create a culture of care and creativity helping the company's bottom line and increasing employee satisfaction.

By encouraging these success factors, employers can help employees develop the skills, knowledge, and attitudes needed to succeed in their roles and contribute to the company's overall success.

The Link Between Success and Belonging

The link between success and belonging is both intricate and powerful, with each shaping and reinforcing the other in dynamic ways. Success can deepen our sense of belonging: when we achieve our goals or gain recognition, we often feel more valued, respected, and part of something bigger than ourselves. This validation strengthens our connection to others who share our values, interests, or experiences, fostering a richer sense of belonging to self and community.

On the other hand, a sense of belonging can help individuals feel more confident, supported, and motivated in pursuing their goals, which can lead to greater success in several ways. First, a sense of belonging can create a supportive and motivating environment that fosters personal and professional growth. When people feel like they are empowered, they have increased confidence. This, in turn, can help individuals perform better and achieve greater success in their roles.

Second, belonging can promote collaboration and innovation, which are essential for success in many workplaces. When people feel like they belong, they are more likely to share ideas, give and receive feedback, and collaborate with others to solve problems and achieve common goals. This can lead to greater creativity, productivity, and effectiveness, which can ultimately contribute to organizational success.

Third, belonging can help individuals build strong networks and relationships, which are valuable for career development and advancement. When people feel like they belong, they are more likely to form connections with colleagues, mentors, and leaders who can offer guidance, support, and opportunities for growth. This can lead to career advancement, increased visibility and recognition, and greater success in the long run.

Braving the Workplace

Braving the workplace means being yourself in a world that tells you to be something different every day. Braving the workplace means showing up as your true self in an environment that constantly pressures you to conform and fit into predefined molds. It's about having the courage to stand in your authenticity, even when it feels risky or uncomfortable. Belonging, true belonging, isn't about fitting in; it's about being accepted for who you are—that includes self-acceptance. When you dare to be yourself, you create space for others to do the same, fostering a culture of genuine connection and inclusion. Remember, belonging only happens when we present our wonderful, imperfect selves to the world; our sense of belonging can never be greater than our level of self-acceptance.

Chapter 4

We're in It Together

Leo Tolstoy noted that happy families are generally happy in the same way, but they are unhappy in many different ways.[18] For a family to be happy, certain key elements must be in place: the good health of all family members, reasonable financial security, and mutual affection. Today, some view the workplace as a kind of surrogate family. While the workplace isn't truly a family, it can feel similar in some ways: it's where we build relationships and shape our social identity. In this chapter, I discuss the importance of understanding that in our workplace, we are all in it together (that being the nature of our social species). Unpacking the implications of how we will be happy and feel like we matter in the same kinds of ways is just as important as understanding how we can feel the opposite in so many different and complex disconnections.

When I was conducting interviews for my dissertation, shit got real. Emotions were high, and since the participants didn't know me, I knew it might be awkward for them to be vulnerable with a stranger (me)—but they were so brave. After I noticed my first participant (we'll call her Christina) struggling with her words, I stopped her and said, "This is a judgment-free zone, and we are in this together." As soon as I said that, something interesting happened—I noticed Christina's pensive body language changed, her tight shoulders dropped, her tears stopped, and she let out a bunch of air. That was an ah-ha moment for me. The phrase "we're in it together" means comfort, a sense of unity, support, and shared responsibility.

"We're in it together" suggests you are not alone in facing challenges or difficult circumstances. It's a reassurance, reminding you that others are experiencing similar struggles. Knowing you are not the only one facing a particular situation can alleviate feelings of isolation and can inspire true belonging and inclusion. It signals that you are part of a community or group that supports and stands by each other. "We're in it together" implies that people are there to offer emotional support and understanding. It reinforces the idea that you can rely on others for comfort, empathy, and encouragement. This support can provide a source of strength and comfort, helping you navigate tough times with a greater sense of resilience. "We're in it together" communicates that everyone involved is accountable and actively working toward a common goal. This shared responsibility can lighten the burden of challenges, helping one become their bravest in the workplace since they don't need to sacrifice themselves on a solo mission as "we're in it together" implies that the load is distributed among a group rather than falling solely on one individual. It fosters a sense of teamwork and cooperation, creating a supportive environment where individuals can rely on each other. Hearing "we're in it together" can provide perspective and reassurance that you are not solely responsible for finding solutions or overcoming obstacles. It reminds you that others are willing to contribute, share their insights, and help find solutions collectively. This shared perspective can alleviate feelings of pressure, uncertainty, and overwhelm.

All About Connection

Want another way to think about the phrase "we're in it together"?
Connection. We're "all-in" to bond, make relationships, or have
associations between ourselves and entities. There are many
types of connection: there's human connection (interpersonal
relationships and connections between individuals), emotional
connection (deep bond formed through shared feelings,
understanding, and mutual empathy), and social connection
(engaging with others in social settings, such as within
communities, groups, or organizations). Connection can also
refer to the ability to relate or comprehend ideas, concepts, or
knowledge. It involves grasping the relationships, patterns, or
relevance of information, which enables deeper understanding
and cognitive integration. In fact, the first part of the definition of
belonging is the innate desire to be part of something larger than
us—connection.

Humans are social creatures, and connection plays a vital role
in our lives, providing a sense of belonging, support, and shared
experiences. Connection contributes to our emotional well-being,
personal growth, and the development of meaningful relationships
and communities. Human connection has biological underpinnings
and is deeply rooted in our biology and neurobiology.

Human connection triggers the release of various neurochemicals
in our brain, such as oxytocin, dopamine, and serotonin. These
chemicals play crucial roles in bonding, social reward, and feelings
of happiness and well-being. Oxytocin is often referred to as
the "love hormone" and is associated with trust, empathy, and
social bonding.

Our brains and bodies are wired to seek and benefit from social interaction and the quality of our connections can have profound effects on our physical and mental health. Connection profoundly impacts stress regulation and our physiological response to stressors. When we feel connected to others, our bodies produce lower levels of stress hormones, such as cortisol, and activate the relaxation response. The presence of social support can buffer the negative effects of stress and contribute to overall well-being. Connection influences the regulation of our autonomic nervous system, which controls bodily functions like heart rate, blood pressure, and digestion. Positive social interactions and emotional connection can activate the parasympathetic nervous system, which is responsible for rest and relaxation, and promote a sense of safety and calm. Social connection and positive social relationships significantly impact our immune system function. Strong social bonds and support have been linked to improved immune response, faster recovery from illness, and better overall health outcomes. Connection is important for our well-being.

The Importance of Professional Connection

Professional connection is established within the context of work or professional settings. It involves building relationships, networking, and collaborating with colleagues, mentors, supervisors, clients, or industry peers to exchange knowledge, support career growth, and achieve common goals. Relationships are crucial for a harmonious work environment and a sense of belonging. Here are some of the workplace relationships that can be formed in a professional setting:

1. **Employee to the company:** A strong connection between employees and the company they work for is characterized by several key elements that foster a positive and meaningful relationship of a lot of parts that make up a whole that make the employee feel a sense of belonging. At the top of the list of those key elements: inclusive and diverse culture, clear and inspiring vision, effective communication, recognition and appreciation, and investment in employee development. When employees feel connected to the company, they are more engaged, motivated, and committed to their work.

2. **Peers and team relationships:** These relationships are built with coworkers who work in the same department or team or maybe even do the same job. This can be coworkers on the same team, different teams in the same organization, or peers from cross-functional teams. This may also be a mentor-mentee relationship where the mentor provides advice, shares knowledge, and helps the mentee develop their skills and career.

3. **Supervisor-subordinate relationships:** This relationship exists between a supervisor or manager and their direct reports. It involves providing guidance, feedback, and performance evaluations. The subordinate contributes effort, skills, and expertise to achieve organizational goals while providing valuable ground-level feedback and fostering trust and cooperation.

4. **Leadership relationships:** This refers to the relationships between leaders within an organization, such as executives, department heads, or team leaders. These relationships involve collaboration, decision-making, and strategic planning to drive the organization's goals and objectives.

Keeping clear boundaries and acting with integrity are key to making workplace relationships work. Respect, honest conversations, and having each other's backs—that's the real foundation for a healthy, productive vibe at work.

Connection to the Company

People find meaning when they see a connection between what they value and what they spend time doing. This goes for all relationships, including the ones we have with our companies. We evaluate the company and our sense of connection in terms of "Do I belong here?" and "Do I want to belong here?" There needs to be a **mutual attraction**, right? Kind of like a romantic relationship—let's run with that. Just as individuals are drawn to each other based on shared interests and values in a romantic relationship, a job seeker may be attracted to a company based on factors such as its mission, culture, reputation, or industry alignment. Next, the courtship begins. The recruitment process can be seen as a **courtship phase**, where both parties engage in a series of interactions to assess compatibility. Similar to being in a romantic relationship, individuals go through a period of getting to know each other, exploring commonalities, and evaluating if they fit each other's needs and expectations. Next, it's important to **establish trust**. Just as individuals in a romantic relationship build trust through open communication, honesty, and shared experiences, employees and employers establish trust through transparent job descriptions, interviews, references, and background checks. In a romantic relationship, commitment is often solidified through an **explicit agreement**, such as marriage or a long-term commitment. Similarly, in an employee-employer relationship, commitment is formalized through a contractual agreement, such as an employment contract or offer letter, outlining the terms and conditions of employment.

After that, there's **growth and development**. The focus shifts to learning and evolving. Both types of relationships center around personal and professional progress. In a romantic relationship, individuals support each other's personal growth and pursue shared goals. Likewise, employers provide opportunities for employees to grow professionally through training, career development programs, and feedback while employees contribute to the growth and success of the company. **Effective communication and collaboration** are essential in both types of relationships. Just as open and clear communication is crucial for resolving conflicts and maintaining a healthy romantic relationship, employees and employers need to communicate effectively to ensure mutual understanding, alignment of expectations, and a positive work environment. Finally, in both scenarios, **long-term satisfaction** is desired. A successful romantic relationship brings happiness, fulfillment, and a sense of belonging, while a satisfying employee-employer relationship offers job satisfaction, career advancement opportunities, a supportive work environment, and a sense of belonging. While employee-employer relationships are primarily professional and centered on work-related goals and expectations, both are typically built on connection and a sense of belonging.

Okay, now for the stuff in between that makes people feel connected and disconnected to the company. In my research, the overwhelming response when I asked participants what made them feel connected to their company was that the company made them **feel part of something bigger than themselves**, part of a community, and that they felt most connected when they didn't have to sacrifice who they are and they could be themselves...put this together and you have the definition of belonging—the *innate human desire to be part of something larger than us without sacrificing who we are*. You can imagine they felt most disconnected when they felt like they had to sacrifice themselves, cover their identities, or just couldn't be themselves.

Disconnected participants mentioned that they felt **the need to fit in** and that it was hard to be themselves. Here are some reasons participants (anonymized via characters from *Buffy the Vampire Slayer*, one of the best TV shows ever) shared for feeling connected or disconnected from the company as it related to their sense of belonging.

"I feel **connected** to the company when...I **share similar values and beliefs** with the company" (Buffy).[19] They feel a stronger sense of alignment, belonging, and connection when the company's mission, vision, and goals resonate with their personal values; it fosters a deeper connection. When the company promotes and lives a positive culture based on belonging and inclusion, they feel more connected. Consequently, they feel **disconnected** from the company when it talks a big game about values and beliefs but doesn't follow through. It's especially disheartening when the company preaches inclusion but holds marginalized employees to a different set of standards.

"I feel **connected** to the company when...I **have opportunities for growth**, specifically when I can learn, grow, and advance within the company" (Willow). Participants shared that access to opportunities made them feel valued, boosting their sense of investment, belonging, and mattering (more on this in a bit). They also said that open, transparent communication from leadership builds trust and deepens their connection to the company. On the flip side, they felt disconnected when opportunities and investment were lacking—it left them feeling stuck, both personally and professionally.

"I feel connected to the company when...the **company provides transparency**" (Xander). When employees feel informed about and, even better, involved in decision-making processes, it promotes a sense of ownership and connection to the company's overall direction. Transparency removes interference and confusion. Looking at this from another angle, participants said that they feel disconnected due to a **lack of transparency and visibility**. One participant said, "I feel disconnected when decisions are made and there's not a lot of explanation given. You have no control and are excluded from the decision-making and conversation. That makes me feel disconnected, then it reminds me, 'Oh yeah, I'm just a number here, nothing more.'"

In the same vein of being or feeling excluded from decision-making, **disconnected** participants also cited that **the company pushed too many priorities**, and as a result, they felt like they could not succeed and it diminished their sense of belonging. For example, one of the leaders expressed frustration and exhaustion around her balance as a leader against the priorities pushed down by the company, citing, "There's been a huge focus on psychological safety and really making sure that we are treating people with compassion and creating a diverse and inclusive environment. While those are values that are important to me, the company seems to have a new purpose each month, and there are lots of balls to juggle. The company expects me to get my job done, execute cultural initiatives that can be time-consuming, and implement a new principle each month" (Cordelia). She expressed that **doing meaningful work made her feel connected** to the company and the "flavor of the month" type of initiatives left her feeling disconnected.

"I feel **connected** to the company when...the **company provides flexibility**" (Giles). Providing flexibility in work arrangements, such as remote work options or flexible schedules, can enhance employees' connection with their company. Providing flexibility made participants feel like the company was meeting them where they were, which increased their sense of belonging. Flexibility demonstrates trust and consideration for work-life balance, which contributes to a positive connection. Participants felt **disconnected** from the company when they felt forced to go into an office, go out for company meetings and social events after hours, and when their **jobs intruded on their personal lives**— typically at night and on weekends.

A combination of shared and lived values, positive culture, meaningful work, supportive relationships, growth opportunities, transparent communication, and workplace flexibility can all contribute to fostering a strong sense of connection and belonging between employees and their company.

Connection to the Team and Workplace Peers

We all have a deep need to belong, to connect, and to feel like part of something larger than us. Similar to belonging to groups, social organizations, tribes, and religious communities, the workplace has the concept of teams. Teams provide social support at work that is emotional, informational, task-oriented, and can be pivotal to, well, just getting through the day. Trust is critical for the success of our relationships with colleagues because it contributes to a sense of belonging in the workplace. There are two kinds of trust within team/peer relationships: conditional and unconditional. Conditional trust is contingent upon certain conditions or specific factors. It is based on a "trust but verify" approach, where trust is given gradually or provisionally, and it may be adjusted depending on the behavior and actions of the other person(s). Unconditional trust, on the other hand, is given freely and wholeheartedly without any specific conditions or prerequisites. It is a deep and unwavering belief in the reliability, integrity, and good intentions of the other person(s).

When unconditional trust is present in relationships, there is an increased sense of belonging, whereas belonging decreases amongst team members because of conditional trust.

Stanley Schachter's "psychology of affiliation" is a theory that explores the motivations behind individuals seeking out and maintaining social relationships. The theory says people are motivated to affiliate with others to satisfy their social needs, such as the need for belonging, companionship, and social support.[20] These affiliative behaviors can be applied to the context of the workplace and shed light on how individuals form connections with teams and peers in that setting. Schachter's theory can also be linked to Henri Tajfel and John Turner's social identity theory,[21] which suggests that individuals derive a part of their self-concept from the groups they belong to. When individuals feel a sense of belonging to their team, it satisfies their need for affiliation, making them more engaged, committed, and motivated to contribute to the team's success. Being part of a team at work shapes how we see ourselves. When we really connect with our team, it boosts our job satisfaction and makes us more committed. Here are sentiments that participants shared about their sense of belonging in relation to their connection with their peers and their team in the workplace.

"I feel **connected** to peers and the team when…I **have positive, meaningful relationships** with colleagues on the immediate and extended teams." When employees build strong connections with their teammates, they're more likely to feel truly part of the team. Participants said they felt **lonely and disconnected when they felt void of relationships**. When they felt lonely, they tended to overcompensate by inviting people out, adding more time to meetings to add chit-chat, striving for a feeling of belonging to combat their loneliness. In addition, participants reported that when they felt lonely, it got harder to speak up for themselves.

One person shared a time when she felt so disconnected from the team that she couldn't find her words—and felt like she couldn't speak up or be herself. She said that the aftermath had drastic consequences: "It was horrible. I didn't sleep very well. I actually gained a lot of weight out of that too. I was in such a state of depression."

"I feel **connected** to peers and the team when...we **bond around non-work-related projects**." In my research, most participants said that they had little contact with peers and teammates beyond projects and they believed that creating more peer-to-peer relationships would increase their sense of connectedness and belonging. They reported that there was little social interaction or moments not tied to work or an outcome the team was all driving toward. Participants expressed displeasure and **disconnection** when there was a **lack of interaction with peers** and thought that more socialization with them would help them bond over non-work-related occasions. One participant told me, "I'm in a constant perpetual state of anxiety and I think that interacting with peers would help me feel like I am not the odd man out. Am I doing too much? Am I doing too little? What are other people doing? What is stressing them out?" He relayed that it would help him feel more connected to build these relationships over non-project-based interactions and that positive interactions increased his sense of belonging.

"I feel connected to peers and the team when...I **feel supported by them**." In the workplace, peers and team members play a crucial role in providing emotional and instrumental support to each other. Positive relationships with peers are the heartbeat of a supportive, collaborative work environment. When people trust each other, they're not just working side by side—they're lifting each other up. In a space like that, you know someone's got your back, and you've got theirs. You can share ideas without fear, ask questions without judgment, and lean on each other when things get tough. It's the kind of connection where people show up fully, ready to help each other succeed—and that's where the real magic happens.

"I feel connected to peers and the team when...**I feel that people know me beyond work**." In my research, one person told me that she felt connected by knowing more about her teammates' lives, and that made her feel connected within the team. She said, "I know all of their kids' names, I get to hear their stories and see pictures from what we did over the weekend or where they traveled on PTO. I feel lucky that we've built deep, personal connections and that I really know them. And that's important to me because we spend so much time together. I need to know them beyond the status updates calls and passing one another in the hallway or a Zoom call." On the flip side, participants told me that when their **peers and teams did not care to learn about them beyond work, they felt disconnected from them**.

Connection to the Company Leadership

We will spend the entire next chapter talking about connection to your direct supervisor, your manager/supervisor—it is critical. Until then, let's explore an important, often overlooked relationship— the one we have with the company's leadership, executives and your hierarchy of leaders.

For individual contributors in the organization, they look to their hierarchy of leaders for change, direction, and inspiration. For managers, they look to their hierarchy of leaders for vision, support, recognition, decision-making, and growth. You may say, *wait, can't both sets of employees want both?* Quick answer—yes, possibly. Is it more nuanced than that? Also, yes. There are many layers of leadership. For our purposes, let's look at the top layer of leadership, executives or company leadership. What do employees want from their executives and what behaviors enhance employee sense of belonging and connection? They want to follow leaders who demonstrate integrity, ethical behavior, and commitment to the company's values and mission, setting a positive example for employees. When leaders embody the qualities they expect from their teams, it strengthens the connection between them and their followers, strengthening the bonds of belonging. Additionally, both types of employees carry the perception of how their executive leaders and their visibility and presence contribute to a sense of belonging in the workplace through connection. Here are sentiments that participants shared about connection as it pertains to their company's leadership.

"I feel **connected to the company's leadership** when...**executives are visionary and promote the company's vision.**" Participants in my research told me that working for a visionary executive team gave them a deep sense of pride, and aligning to the vision that they promoted gave them a deep, positive connection. They especially like when leaders weave the vision and methods of how to achieve said vision into ongoing company communications and show progress against the vision with consistency. Participants reported feeling **disconnected when executives promote the vision, but they don't take it to reality**. Participants say that when the vision is not actualized it feels like it is all for optics—in other words, talk is cheap. When a visionary leader drops the ball—when they don't follow through on their promise and don't guide their leaders to make it real—it's like a crack in the foundation. Trust starts to erode, and that sense of connection? It slips away. People feel the disconnect, and it's hard to rebuild what's been lost. Getting that trust back isn't impossible, but it takes more than words—it takes showing up again and again, proving that this time, things will be different.

"I feel **connected to the company's leadership** when...**executives reinforce values**." Participants had a higher sense of belonging and deeper connection with the company's leadership when the executive team reinforced company values and employees believed that their values were aligned to the company's values, strengthening their sense of belonging. One participant told me, "Every year, our executive team reinforces our company values and I feel myself feeling a deep alignment to those values. It restores my faith in the company and that I belong here." On the contrary, employees feel **disconnected when the values are aspirational** and—similar to vision—when the executives don't take that aspiration to reality.

"I feel **connected to the company's leadership** when...**executives lead by example**." One participant told me that the example of leadership stems from the top. "It starts with our CEO. He leads by example. He's the first one to say, 'Thank you.'" They continued, "I mean, the philanthropy work that he does speaks for itself. Our executives learn from him and they are visible and encouraging, on a weekly basis."

When employees feel connected to executives, they are more engaged in their work. Engaged employees are passionate about their roles, committed to the organization's goals, and willing to go the extra mile to contribute to its success.

Sense of Mattering

When people feel connected—to the company, to their peers, to leadership—they don't just feel like they belong; they feel like they matter. And let's be real: feeling like we matter isn't just a nice-to-have—it's a fundamental human need and a vital part of our well-being. A sense of mattering is closely tied to feelings of belonging, purpose, and self-worth. When individuals know their contributions are valued, it lights them up. They're more motivated, engaged, and ready to show up fully in their work and personal lives, bringing their best ideas forward, taking risks, and investing deeply because they feel like they're part of something that genuinely values them.

But when people feel invisible—like their efforts go unnoticed or their presence doesn't make a difference—it's isolating, leading to feelings of loneliness, low self-esteem, and a sense of disconnection from their purpose. A lack of mattering has real consequences.

We want to feel that we matter, both to ourselves and others. Personal significance to self is hard to achieve. It's a lifelong quest—c'mon, you know how hard we are on ourselves. The feeling of mattering is closely tied to an individual's self-esteem and self-worth. When people experience positive connections and relationships, it boosts their self-esteem, reinforcing the belief that they are valued members of the group or organization. We experience it through meaningful interactions and relationships with others. Through these interactions, individuals experience a sense of personal significance. When people feel heard, understood, and valued in their interactions, they are more likely to believe that they matter and that their opinions and feelings are respected. When individuals feel connected to others or to an organization, they experience a sense of belonging, where they believe they are an integral part of the group or organization and their presence is valued.

In the workplace, a sense of mattering can be fostered through a variety of practices, such as providing opportunities for employees to contribute their ideas and perspectives, recognizing and rewarding employees for their achievements, and creating a culture of inclusion and collaboration. When employees feel that they matter and that their contributions are valued, they are more likely to feel engaged and committed to their work and to be more productive and effective in their roles. Connection with others provides a form of social validation. When people connect and interact positively with peers, colleagues, or leaders, they receive positive reinforcement and recognition. This validation reinforces their sense of mattering, as they perceive that their actions and contributions are recognized and appreciated by others.

Overall, the sense of mattering is deeply intertwined with connecting and forming meaningful relationships with others and is a strong component of our sense of belonging. While sense of mattering isn't just about belonging, it's a big part. It's knowing your absence would be felt—and missed. It's being valued and appreciated for being you. When individuals feel connected, supported, and valued, it strengthens their belief that they matter within their social circles, teams, or workplaces. Conversely, a lack of connection or isolation can lead to feelings of insignificance or a diminished sense of mattering. Therefore, fostering positive connections and a sense of belonging is essential for promoting a strong sense of mattering among individuals in various contexts. In connected environments, people often experience support and empathy from others. Feeling supported and understood reinforces their sense of mattering, as they recognize that their well-being and emotions are cared for by others.

Let's break for a little introspection around a sense of mattering.

Describe a time where the workplace increased your sense of mattering. The criteria are that you felt valued, important to others, and that your contributions were recognized and appreciated.

_____

_____

_____

_____

_____

Tell me what in life you can't live without—what means the most to you?

_____

_____

_____

_____

_____

How about things that you can't live without related to work (putting the paycheck aside and of course the coffee station)? About/from your company? About/from your peers? About/from your leadership?

_____

_____

_____

_____

_____

I'm curious, are there similarities between what you can't live without in workplaces and the rest of your life? Differences? Are you sacrificing one for the other (if so, why?)?

The Rise of Employee Resource Groups

One of the ways that the workplace fosters the "we're in it together" feeling to form a connected environment and increased sense of belonging through Employee Resource Groups (ERGs). ERGs are voluntary workplace groups made up of employees who share a common characteristic, demographic, life stage, function, or other shared identity or interest. ERGs are sometimes also known as Affinity Groups or Business Resource Groups (BRGs). Whatever name they go by, ERGs serve as platforms for employees to connect, support one another, and advocate for their shared interests within the organization. ERGs often organize events, workshops, and development programs that cater to the specific needs and interests of their members. These opportunities for learning and growth can boost employee engagement and job satisfaction.

ERGs can vary significantly both between different companies and within the same company. The nature of employees with diverse

backgrounds, experiences, and ideas can lead to a wide range of
ERGs, each with its unique focus and mission. ERGs are admirable
in their intent to give a voice to underrepresented individuals,
celebrate diversity, and promote belonging in the workplace.

Companies promote ERGs to inspire belonging at work in several
ways in addition to what has already been mentioned:

1.   By promoting ERGs, companies demonstrate their
     commitment to inclusivity and diversity, creating an
     environment where employees feel respected and valued
     for their unique identities.

2.   ERGs provide a space for employees to have their voices
     heard and advocate for their needs within the organization.
     This empowerment and representation contribute to a
     sense of belonging, as employees know they have a platform
     to influence positive change.

3.   Demonstrating a commitment to fostering a sense of
     belonging through ERGs can positively impact recruitment
     and retention efforts. Prospective employees are attracted
     to organizations that value diversity and inclusion, while
     current employees are more likely to stay in an inclusive and
     supportive environment.

4.   ERGs provide employees with a sense of community. Being
     part of a group that shares similar journeys or backgrounds
     fosters a supportive and understanding atmosphere,
     helping employees feel like they belong and they are
     not alone in their experiences. These groups provide a
     supportive network where employees can seek advice, share
     knowledge, and build professional relationships that can
     enhance their career growth.

5.   Employee well-being is so important and ERGs address
     various aspects including mental health, work-life balance,

and overall job satisfaction. By supporting these groups, companies prioritize their employees' overall happiness and fulfillment at work.

So, if ERGs are as magical as I've described above, are they the answer to the belonging issue? Not quite—but not so far off either. ERGs often at least partially fulfill each of these purposes and goals, but they have their drawbacks, too. When members of ERGs are with their ERGs, they may have a false feeling that diversity issues have been solved across the company due to a strong sense of belonging to their ERGs. It may give them the false hope that everyone in the company sees their challenges the way that the ERGs see them. Workplace bravery in this case is speaking up to connect ERGs back to the company with actions associated to make it easier to navigate the workplace. Yet, when that doesn't feel doable and members of ERGs experience a partial sense of belonging to the group, they've reported feeling belonging uncertainty that negatively impacted their propensity to thrive in the workplace.

One Big Happy Family

Have you ever referred to your coworkers as family? I can admit it, I have said it quite a few times. In fact, it gave me a huge sense of pride. That could be because the family I came from left me feeling less than...well, just less than. So, when a company told me that they would be my new family, some part deep down inside felt a gap may be filled. It makes sense that I would feel that way because today's companies have infused the workplace with familism once found in the traditional family structures (and we spend approximately one-third of our life "at work"). There are tons of people like me out there (maybe you're like me in this, too) that didn't come from Norman Rockwell-like families or even healthy ones, and it makes sense why a company calling themselves a family sounds like a dream come true—finally, a place to belong. I mean, I just spent thousands of words talking to you about connection and the chapters before that telling you that we spend most of our waking hours at work. Sure, the workplace isn't family—but in some ways, it can feel a lot like one. It's where we build connections, find belonging, and shape a big part of who we are. The relationships we form at work don't just bind us to a job; they connect us to each other in ways that run deep.

Today, the workplace has become, for some, a surrogate family. While the sentiment of work being a family is seemingly positive, calling the workplace a family has both confused people and allowed them to remove themselves from more traditional institutions of belonging. And just like the families we all grew up in, they all take on different shapes and forms. One of the participants I met with in my research told me that she believed that the term "family" is aspirational, both helpful and harmful— helpful in the way that everyone wants to be cared for and harmful in the way that family means something different to each employee from different countries and cultures. She told me, "The goal is to create an environment that sort of wraps you up in a warm hug and that we care for each other and about each other. It's a way to bring people into the fold. Family is about how the company expects you to act, treat your fellow colleagues and employees with care...this is like having an extended big family and you're probably close to some and not close to others."

Some employees enjoy workplace familism. One even told me, "I extend the same care for my work family as I do my real family. I treat my team like family, and I tell them we are a family. I feel like I'm a dad to them. They come to me with issues, and I give coaching on how to resolve them. I treat them with the same care that I give my kids; that is how important my work family is to me.

We spend more time with each other than we probably do with our families."

Others are simply not down with the concept: "My family is my family, and the workplace family is nice in theory but seriously makes me cringe. People take it so seriously and it really messes you up mentally throughout your career if you let it."

So, what happens when employees aren't down with the "family" identity that their company is serving up? Do the employees speak up? The overwhelming response from my participants was *nope*. Here is an example that was conveyed to me: "I don't dare speak up and voice my opinion that I am not aligned with family as a company value. It becomes so personal to people and when engaged in the conversation on company values, they say it feels personal, they will say the CEO is family. In reality, we don't know the CEO like you know our family and I think the company perpetuates this confusion and plays on people's emotions and sense of family."

Another response that resonated came from a tenured employee explaining why the concept of workplace familism negatively impacted her sense of belonging. She told me, "My real family is my family, not the people I work with. Would I tell any of my coworkers that? No way. That would be almost blasphemous since we are a culture that has spent, you know, a couple of decades now, you know, trying to foster a family vibe and leaders are almost seen as parents. It's the same with purpose. I love what I do but make no mistake, it's for a paycheck."

Speaking up against the family concept has become taboo and is clearly uncomfortable. For many companies, the extent of effort spent addressing employee woes and concerns around vulnerability to speak up around "family" has been to say, "We are family, so you belong." Unlike saying, "We are in it together" and showing actions to prove that you will be a partner in their care and belongingness, this response ignores—and may even be a way of suppressing—some pretty legitimate employee concerns. Merely proclaiming to employees, "We are like a family, and you belong here!" overlooks their valid concerns and can even put the burden on the employees themselves. By effectively saying, "We've assured you of your belonging, so if you still feel uncertain, it's your issue to deal with," the company risks dismissing the genuine feelings of the employees. *Stop* telling employees, "We are family, you belong."

People managers at companies with family as part of their core values and culture (you can guess what role they play in the family: Mom or Dad) told me about the detrimental ways that familism is playing out in the workplace, with unintended consequences. One mentioned, "As a leader, I cannot tell you how many hurt feelings and issues I've had to deal with because employees are searching for this perfect image of family at work." He went on to say managers are not equipped to manage these issues and when companies pursue familism, they face performance issues like low engagement and high attrition. In addition, misunderstandings arise due to the differences between perceptions of what family means to employees versus how it is or is not actualized by the company, and then direct managers are left holding the bag on belonging uncertainty and exclusion.

Belonging Uncertainty and Exclusion While We Are Supposed to Be in It Together

So, what happens when the concept of family, meant to be a positive sentiment in the workplace, leads to feelings and emotions of negativity and potentially thwarted belonging? Belonging uncertainty can manifest itself in several ways. For example, if an individual is new to a workplace or team, they may be uncertain about whether they will be accepted by their colleagues. Similarly, if an individual is facing a significant change in their personal or professional life, such as a job relocation, a demotion, promotion, changing teams, etc., they may be uncertain about how their social networks will change and whether they will be able to find a sense of belonging in their new environment. When employees find themselves going against the grain of a company's cultural norm like familism, or when the lines between work and life start to blur, uncertainty and exclusion may set in.

When individuals experience belonging uncertainty, it can create a "social pain" that activates similar neural pathways in the brain as physical pain. It hurts, and you are black and blue on the inside—which is harder for others to notice. Social pain can lead to feelings of stress, anxiety, and depression, and can negatively impact an individual's mental and emotional well-being, and we know that thwarted belonging is frequently an antecedent to suicide—the pain doesn't get any more real than that. While I realize that everything pales in comparison to suicide, social pain and experiences associated may also lead to decreased self-esteem, increased social isolation, and a sense of alienation—the gateway to thwarted belonging and suicide.

When people experience exclusion or even perceived exclusion it feels like rejection. It feels like someone or something is telling us we are not enough. For some, it feels like, "No, not you. I choose not to care about or even tolerate you." It runs deep for all of us, even the ones that tell you it doesn't bother them. Trust me, it does. We all have the tendency to overthink and obsess over not feeling included, chosen, and wanted. Sometimes it fits into the narrative of the story we tell ourselves of not being enough, not worthy—all the shoulds, coulds, woulds. The "story we tell ourselves" can be dangerous because it shapes our perceptions, beliefs, and actions, influencing how we interpret events and experiences. When we construct a narrative in our minds, we tend to filter information to fit that narrative. To counter the dangers of "the story we tell ourselves," we have to practice real self-awareness and challenge the narratives running in our heads. It's about catching ourselves in those moments and asking, "Is this true, or is this just my story?" Grounding ourselves in reality takes work—and trust me, it's way easier said than done. But it's the only way to keep our stories from taking us places we don't need to go.

The link between belonging uncertainty and exclusion is closely tied to how individuals perceive their identity (again, the story we tell ourselves) and their place within a particular group like a team or community or company. Belonging uncertainty refers to the feeling of uncertainty or doubt about whether one truly belongs or is accepted. Exclusion, on the other hand, refers to being left out, rejected, or marginalized within all aspects in the workplace. Belonging uncertainty can lead to feelings of anxiety, stress, and self-doubt. When individuals are unsure of their belongingness, they may constantly question their acceptance and worry about potential rejection or exclusion. People experiencing belonging uncertainty are more susceptible to feelings of exclusion. This vulnerability stems from their heightened sensitivity to social cues and actions that may signal rejection or distancing from the team, their peers, managers, the company, and so on. Here are some additional ways belonging uncertainty and exclusion are experienced together in the workplace:

- **Confirmation bias:** Belonging uncertainty may lead individuals to interpret ambiguous or neutral social interactions as evidence of exclusion. They may be more likely to perceive slights or ignore positive cues, reinforcing their feelings of not belonging.

- **Reduced participation:** The fear of exclusion may lead individuals with belonging uncertainty to withdraw or reduce their participation in group activities. This behavior, often driven by the desire to avoid potential rejection, can further reinforce a sense of exclusion.

- **Influence on group dynamics:** In group settings, individuals experiencing belonging uncertainty may be perceived as less integrated or invested in the group's goals. This perception can inadvertently contribute to their exclusion from group decision-making and activities.

- **Diminished job satisfaction:** In the workplace, employees who feel uncertain about their belongingness may experience reduced job satisfaction and engagement. This can lead to higher turnover rates and lower team cohesion, affecting overall organizational performance.

Navigating feelings of belonging and the constant worry of being left out isn't easy, but it's absolutely crucial for our well-being. When we're wrapped in the certainty that we are valued, seen, and supported, that's where we find a true sense of belonging. But when we're uncertain, feeling like we're one misstep away from exclusion, that's tough on the soul.

One way to ease this is to surround yourself with the people and spaces that let you be your full self—just as you are. And sometimes, the best place to do this isn't at work but outside of it. Try joining a group, volunteering, or diving into a hobby that lights you up. Seek out those places where you can show up fully and feel connected just for being you. It's in these supportive, outside-of-work circles that we can find steady ground and remember who we truly are.

What supportive networks and/or activities outside of the workplace bring you moments of belonging that bring you back to you?

_____

_____

_____

_____

_____

_____

For me, it's music and travel. Music is nostalgic for me and makes me remember who I am—away from other people's perceptions. More specifically, away from the people who will want me to feel better and may not be as objective as I'd like. And travel gives me a sense of newness and adventure and makes me feel part of something much bigger than me, which checks the true belonging box.

Chapter 5

It's About the Managers

At four feet six inches, the Artful Dodger was the top dog manager
for his 1830s employer in the classic Dickens novel *Oliver Twist*.[22]
The Artful Dodger was a remarkable manager not because he was
a charismatic orator (he wasn't) nor a master of strategic planning
(not even close), but because he was simply the best pickpocket
in town, and in spite of his size his esteemed managerial status
made him seem larger than life. Yet, there was something else
about the Artful Dodger's approach to management that set
him apart from the rest. He understood the power of providing a
simple meal and a place to eat to the poor youths of London. In
doing so, he gained not only their loyalty but also their unwavering
commitment to his cause with an unspoken understanding that
they belonged with him. Now, before we draw any hasty parallels
between Dickens' tale and the modern corporate world, the focus
in this chapter illuminates the power that managers have over
their employees, highlighting the notion that good leadership
requires more than merely reading a book or taking an on-demand
course on leadership—particularly when seen through the lens of
belongingness in the workplace.

So, dear readers and leaders (inclusive of all people managers),
let us take a cue from the unlikeliest of figures in Dickens' classic
tale. Let us recognize the influence we hold over the lives of those
we lead and the power we have to foster a sense of belonging

in the workplace. And in doing so, let us lead with the artfulness of compassion, care, empathy, and a genuine understanding of the human experience. For it is through these qualities that we can truly transform our teams and our organizations, ensuring a brighter and more united future for all.

I've told you already, I am good at burying the lede, so...to break that habit I'll come right out with it: **the manager has the biggest influence on the sense of belonging in the workplace**. Phew, I have been waiting an entire chapter to tell you that. Are you surprised? No? Not even a little? Let's dive into what the role of the people manager is and just why they are so important to our sense of belonging at work and beyond.

First, a little level setting. What is the role of a people manager? To me, it is all about coaching and growing, leaving people better than you found them. A people leader, also known as a manager or supervisor, plays a crucial role in overseeing and leading a team of employees within an organization. They help employees navigate their careers and the organization. Managers should focus on supporting employees by removing obstacles and interference and meeting them where they are. By doing this, they help create a clearer path toward a strong sense of belonging. When looking for the standard set of responsibilities of the job, it turns out there isn't one...there are a lot of lists but no standards. So, allow me to set the standard of what I believe to be, well, the table stakes of the job.

- **Team leadership and development:** One of the key responsibilities of a people manager is leading and developing their team. This involves offering guidance, direction, and coaching to direct reports, helping them navigate their roles and responsibilities effectively. Part of said leadership is to cultivate a positive and inclusive work environment that promotes both safety and professional growth. Providing opportunities for personal and career development is paramount, as it empowers team members to reach their full potential. This involves identifying and eliminating any potential interferences, allowing your direct reports to concentrate on their core tasks and objectives without unnecessary distractions. This proactive approach ensures that everyone can contribute effectively toward the team's collective goals.

- **Hiring and onboarding:** You can't have a team without hiring people (unless you inherit them)—after all, you need followers to be a leader. People managers actively participate in the recruitment and selection of new team members, playing a pivotal role in identifying and bringing in top talent. Once hired, it is the responsibility of the people manager to ensure that their new hires are onboarded. Onboarding is one of the most influential belonging moments in an employee's career with the company because it sets the initial tone for their experience, shapes their perceptions of the organization's culture, and establishes a foundation for a sense of belonging and integration within the team and broader company. Some companies have fancy onboarding programs, some don't—regardless, the goal is to facilitate a smooth integration for new hires, helping them acclimate to both the team and the broader organization. By effectively managing these stages, a people manager contributes significantly to building a strong, cohesive, and high-performing team.

- **Goal-setting, planning, and execution:** Goal-setting, planning, and execution—oh my! This means inspiring collaboration amongst team members, as well as cross-teams, to establish and align individual and collective goals with the broader objectives and mission of the organization.

Additionally, a people manager is responsible for effective task delegation, considering the unique strengths and skills of each team member. This ensures that responsibilities are allocated optimally, maximizing productivity and efficiency. Finally, managers oversee the allocation of budgets, equipment, and resources dedicated to the team in the organization, ensuring that they are managed judiciously to support the team's objectives.

- **Performance management and improvement:** A key responsibility of a people manager lies in the realm of performance management and improvement. This involves conducting thorough evaluations of individual and team performance, offering constructive feedback, and setting clear expectations for their professional growth. Additionally, the people manager takes charge of conducting formal performance evaluations and assists employees in setting meaningful goals. They should keenly identify areas where team members may benefit from additional training or support. In such cases, the people manager provides valuable coaching and resources to aid them in making necessary course corrections, ensuring continuous progress and development within the team. By effectively managing performance, a people manager contributes significantly to the overall success of the team and the organization—and helps to grow their team members to achieve their full potential.

- **Performance metrics and reporting:** Managing people performance metrics and reporting entails the vigilant monitoring and reporting of team performance in relation to key performance indicators (KPIs) and other pertinent metrics. By keeping a close eye on these crucial indicators, the people manager gains valuable insights into both individual and team effectiveness and ensures that progress aligns with organizational goals and objectives. This information forms a cornerstone for informed decision-making and strategic planning, ultimately contributing to the team's overall success.

- **Conflict resolution, decision-making, and policy adherence and enforcement:** Arguably the least fun part of the job, the people manager shoulders the responsibility of conflict resolution, decision-making, policy adherence, and enforcement within the team. This entails acting as a mediator in cases of conflicts or disputes among team members, ensuring that resolutions are reached that preserve a harmonious work environment. Additionally, the manager plays a pivotal role in making decisions related to team goals, project priorities, and resource allocation, striking a balance between the needs of the team and the broader objectives of the organization. They are expected to toe the company's party lines, upholding adherence to policies, procedures, and the code of conduct, thereby fostering a culture of compliance and accountability within the team.

- **Communication:** A huge part of the job of people managers is to ensure that communication is both clear and effective, serving as a bridge between upper management and team members—and between themselves and their team members. Types of communication vary and may look like:

  - Providing constructive feedback on performance, highlighting strengths and areas for improvement.

  - Holding regular one-on-one meetings with team members to address individual concerns, provide coaching, and offer support.

  - Setting boundaries to establish a framework for appropriate behavior and interactions.

- **Change management:** People look to their leaders in times of change, so it's no surprise that change management is table stakes. Change management entails providing guidance and support during periods of change, whether it be reorganizations, process improvements, or the introduction of new initiatives. The people manager plays a key role in ensuring that the team adapts smoothly to these shifts, helping team members navigate challenges and embrace new directions. Through effective change management, the manager contributes to the team's agility and resilience in the face of evolving circumstances, ultimately driving the organization toward success. Leaders should take to heart these wise words from change experts Jean Kantambu Latting and V. Jean Ramsey: "People do not resist change, they resist being changed. People want to change on their own terms, not someone else's."[23] Effective leaders will focus on involving their team in the change process, providing clear communication, and empowering employees to take ownership of their roles in the new environment. By doing so, they can foster a sense of agency and collaboration, making the transition smoother and more acceptable for everyone involved.

So, those are what I view as basic table stakes. You may come up with more than I did; that's cool. I've already argued that people managers also have a responsibility for the well-being of their employees as well—as part of these table stakes. Let's dig in deeper.

The Role That People Managers Play in Employee Well-Being

Overall, a people manager is responsible for creating an environment where team members can thrive, meet their goals, and contribute effectively to the organization's success. They're the heartbeat of team performance, shaping not just how we work but how we feel about coming to work every day. And here's the real kicker: they play a huge role in our well-being. When leaders show up with empathy and support, it doesn't just make for a better workday—it makes a real impact on our lives. We all know that people managers have the power to create a positive or negative work environment. Their leadership style, communication, decision-making, and overall conduct significantly influence whether the workplace is positive, supportive, and productive or if it leans toward negativity, stress, and dissatisfaction among team members. What we rarely talk about is that their impact goes way beyond our nine-to-five.

When you have a bad day at work, does it ever spill beyond five o'clock when you metaphorically (or literally) punch out? Stress stemming from our work can manifest in various ways. That sinking feeling before a presentation, that competitive coworker who always needs to one-up you, the never-ending rumor mill… and let's not forget, that tense interaction with a manager who leaves you feeling uncertain or undervalued. These experiences have a way of staying with us long after work hours.

A sense of belonging at work is not confined to the office; it has the potential to positively impact various aspects of an employee's personal life. Feeling like you belong at work can positively affect your overall mental and emotional well-being.

This satisfaction can spill over into your personal life, making you more content and fulfilled overall. It can reduce stress and anxiety, leading to better mental and physical health overall. Conversely, having a good day at work can indeed raise serotonin levels in individuals. Serotonin is a neurotransmitter that plays a crucial role in regulating mood, happiness, and overall well-being. Elevated serotonin levels can improve mood, enhance focus, and increase overall feelings leading to greater productivity and job satisfaction.

People managers wield an extraordinary influence on the mental health of employees, rivaling the impact of therapists, doctors, and even spouses and partners. Their role goes way beyond just getting the work done; they play a huge part in the well-being and quality of life of their team. And it makes sense, right? We spend so much of our lives at work, so it's only natural that how we feel about it—and who's leading us—has a big impact on our mental health.

Picture your brain as a DJ in the booth, mixing tracks of motivation, focus, and mood to keep the energy going. Now, think of your manager as the club owner, who can either make or break the vibe, leaving you counting down the hours. When managers bring positive energy to the table—recognizing hard work, supporting growth, and building trust—they're basically turning up the volume on your brain's reward pathways. These pathways are like the dopamine dance floor, where dopamine, our brain's "feel-good" neurotransmitter, gets everyone moving. Dopamine hands out little mental high-fives, making us feel motivated and satisfied. At the same time, serotonin, the brain's "chill but happy" track, keeps our mood steady. When managers provide an environment where we feel accomplished and appreciated, serotonin kicks in, creating a mood lift that lasts long after closing time.

Now, let's talk about what happens when the club owner goes rogue: cue the cortisol playlist. Cortisol, the brain's stress hormone, is what spins when a manager micromanages, overlooks support, or keeps the environment tense. Too much of it can turn our little DJ into a bundle of nerves, losing the beat on well-being. The stress-heavy playlist messes with the dopamine and serotonin grooves, hijacking the feel-good tunes with anxious beats and leaving us mentally drained. Managers who show care, empathy, and communicate effectively tap into neural circuits for trust and collaboration, cranking up a positive workplace culture. When managers understand the neuroscience of well-being, they're not just setting a good vibe—they're crafting a space where creativity, focus, and collaboration come naturally, turning the workplace into a hit night after night.

Just like a DJ sets the vibe for the dance floor, a manager shapes the workplace rhythm—but there's more to it than just good beats and positive energy. Beneath the surface, our brains are wired for something deeper: a sense of belonging. Belonging constitutes a powerful survival instinct, with managers often underestimating its significance in the workplace. Neglecting this fundamental need can trigger adverse physical and emotional reactions, likely manifesting as discomfort, distress, and mental/physical pain. The inherent hypervigilance to navigate social isolation ingrained in our nervous system over centuries may resurface, detrimentally affecting our capacity to engage effectively within a team environment, hindering collaboration, innovation, and communication.

Employees today feel overlooked when it comes to their mental well-being in the workplace. One in three individuals express disappointment in their manager's failure to acknowledge their contributions, while nearly three in four report that work-related stress spills over into their personal lives, casting a shadow on their home lives. Notably, a substantial two-thirds of respondents indicate a willingness to sacrifice financial gain for a position that prioritizes their mental wellness.

For the sake of more knowledge, here are some quick red flags for all of you leaders out there generally curious about how you may or may not be contributing to a toxic culture (and some validation for the individual contributors, I see you).

- **Lack of clarity in expectations:** Leaders who don't clearly communicate goals, expectations, and guidelines can cause confusion and a lack of direction amongst team members, fostering a culture where initiative and risk-taking are discouraged.

- **Tolerance of toxic behavior:** Leaders who overlook toxic conduct within the team risk normalizing such behavior, leading to lowered morale, decreased trust, and reduced cooperation among team members.

- **Preferential treatment:** Leaders who display favoritism toward specific team members can breed resentment and division within the team, hindering collaboration and effective teamwork.

- **Excessive workload:** Leaders who impose unrealistic work hours, deadlines, and demands contribute to burnout and dissatisfaction among team members, creating an unhealthy work-life balance.

- **Lack of feedback:** Leaders who neglect to provide regular feedback, both positive and constructive, can make team members feel undervalued and unacknowledged, fostering a culture of disengagement and apathy.

- **Disregard for team contributions:** Leaders who dismiss the input and ideas of their team members create

an environment where individuals feel marginalized
and unimportant, resulting in reduced motivation
and participation.

All of this impacts a company, and while important, I also need to
point out how it impacts us on a personal, human level—you need
to get it; people's lives are on the line.

Dismissal of negative emotions, pressure to be positive,
invalidation of feelings. The list goes on and on. While I believe
no manager goes into leadership to fuck up people's lives, they
need to know that relationships with leadership have the biggest
impact on an employee's sense of belonging, so when managers
ignore, mistreat, or confuse them, it seriously messes them up.

In my research, participants told me countless stories of how
their managers impacted their well-being. One still haunts me.
Christina told me how much trauma she experienced at the hands
of a prior manager and how, ten years later, she is still suffering
from that manager via post-traumatic stress in several ways: she
has recurring nightmares, she cuts herself, she gained weight,
and she has tried to take her life. She told me, "When I stopped
and I thought to myself of my top ten list of bad things that have
happened to me in life, this person is at the top of my list. And
when you compare that to my list, including the death of my
husband, that's pretty bad. This leader, she yelled at people, but
then like an hour later, she tried to act like your best friend."

She described how this manager marginalized everyone, how she
gaslit them, and made them slowly feel like they were losing their
minds and, frankly, didn't belong. Christina told me about the
shame that she has that this manager still has this impact on her
ten years later. She said it was an awful time and continues to be,
but it wasn't always that bad. When her manager took over the
team, everyone "loved" her. They threw her a one-year anniversary

party and after, she started to distance herself. Her boss was going through a rough breakup and after, her boss became unbearable. The team was never the same and Christina was never the same as she questioned herself and their relationship, experienced suicidal ideation, and lost her sense of belonging at work.

As I mentioned before, I too was haunted by a former manager that I had not worked for in ages, and because of those interactions and that dysfunctional relationship, I was suicidal. I felt like those around me would be better off without me, like I was a burden to others and to myself, like people didn't care about me the way I cared about them, and like there was no place for me left in the world. That's because a sense of belonging can be a protective factor for mental well-being and when it was lost, when I didn't feel connected to others, didn't feel valued, and felt isolated and worthless, it increased my vulnerability to mental health challenges that I didn't know how to deal with or give words to—until I did. My manager was a grade-A narcissist, and I tried several things with him. Sometimes I tried to appeal to his goals and make it all about him. I was fawning over him as a trauma response—a behavior where individuals excessively people-please, appease, or comply with others to avoid conflict and ensure safety, often stemming from a history of trauma or abuse. I would aim to gain approval and prevent further harm by prioritizing his needs over mine. Other times I tried to avoid him. When I did have to talk to him, I kept the conversations short, telling him it was to "give him time back" when knowing that I would need to talk to him would give me painful stomachaches and massive anxiety.

I had duck syndrome: I seemed calm and composed gliding on the water but underneath the surface I worked hard to pedal my feet to stay afloat in what felt like shark-infested waters, and so no one around me was any wiser. Outwardly, I projected an image of competence and success while, internally, I experienced stress, pressure, and emotional struggles and was suicidal. I was dealing with major internal struggles not immediately visible and therefore decided that I was too good at hiding and that must be why my manager was so dismissive, uncaring, and disconnected. So, I decided to tell him (as described in Chapter 1). I told my manager I was suicidal, and that narcissistic asshole did me the best favor of all time—he did nothing. It was then and there that I snapped out of my mental state of workplace torture and got out of dodge.

So, if my manager had promoted a healthy work-life balance and positive environment, would I have felt better about him? Yes, that would have helped. The manager's pursuit of promoting a healthy work-life balance is half the battle—actually, it's more like a thirty-seventy split. Modeling the right behavior and actualizing it is far more important to employees, "walk the walk" and all. If he had promoted a more positive environment, collaborated with me, and cooperated with me, then yes, it would have meant a lot. If he would have valued me for more than my achievements to the company's bottom line—it would have helped. Had he set expectations with me and known what mattered to me, I would have felt psychologically safe and that would have helped.

How about if he would have given me more autonomy? Hard pass since I barely spoke to him, so autonomy came with ignoring me. I didn't need space and flexibility; quite the opposite, I wanted him to be involved and present with me. When employees don't hear from their managers, uncertainty can set in and then comes avoidance. When an employee doesn't hear from their manager for a while, avoidance behavior may set in due to several reasons. First, the lack of communication can lead to uncertainty and anxiety about the employee's performance, status, or future within the organization. Without clear guidance or feedback from their manager, employees may feel directionless and unsure about how to proceed with their work tasks or projects. Additionally, the absence of communication from the manager may create a perception of being undervalued or overlooked, leading to feelings of demotivation and disengagement. As a result, employees may avoid reaching out to their manager or addressing issues proactively, fearing negative repercussions or a lack of responsiveness.

Overall, the absence of communication can erode trust, collaboration, and morale within the team, ultimately fostering avoidance behavior among employees. My manager's lack of contact with me was seen by me as him "trusting" me, and this is all too common. Absentee managers disguise neglect as trust. Want to hear something hilarious? Optically speaking, everyone thought I was his favorite—that's how well I hid this shit and how toxic he was—while secretly, he was beating me down behind closed doors.

So, aside from the obvious things, like modeling the right behaviors (e.g., not working all hours of the day and not expecting the same of their employees), acting with kindness and professionalism, and respecting one another, here are some of the more non-obvious things that managers can do to promote positive well-being in the workplace:

1. **Set clear expectations**. Ensure that employees have a clear understanding of their roles and expectations.

2. **Treat each employee as unique and individual**. Seek to understand the unique needs of each team member and tailor support and coaching accordingly to them. For example: Jess believes that her value and what makes her unique is her expertise in product launches and that is her power and pride—when you go to other people for her expertise around product launches, she feels belonging uncertainty—like she doesn't matter as much. Same goes for the way people like to be acknowledged. Remember that not everyone likes to receive praise the same way. For example, some enjoy private praise and others public.

3. **Get to know who your employees are both inside and outside of the workplace**. That doesn't mean you become close friends or even hang out outside work. It means getting to know what is important to one another. Learn about their home life without being intrusive. Learn what matters to them: their history, what makes them proud, their values, what keeps them up at night, and aspects of their family culture. And please, stop scheduling work events and meetings over their holidays—even if the company remains open on those days.

4. **Learn what type of belonging bucket they fall into**. Do they have true, thwarted, sacrificial, or dissimulated belonging? They may not even know themselves, so asking them straight up may do nothing more than confuse them. Instead, introduce them to the different types of belonging from Chapter 1 and see what resonates most with them (more on this in Chapter 6).

5. **Create opportunities for social connection and personal development during work hours**. Trust me, not everyone wants to stay after for a happy hour or a dinner—and if you have remote employees this could alienate them.

6. **Recognize birthdays and work anniversaries**. By now, most of us have reminders—set a reminder. It may seem trivial—it's not. You have no idea how many belonging conversations start with, "It may sound silly but when my manager forgot my anniversary it hurt my feelings and damaged how I saw her/him."

7. **Allow for failure**. Employees who are allowed to fail and learn from their mistakes develop resilience. When we step outside our comfort zones and take risks, failure becomes an inevitable part of the process. Make it acceptable and share experiences of where you failed as well. They can learn from your failures too.

When an employee feels genuinely appreciated and valued in the workplace, it becomes a cornerstone for fostering positive well-being. Recognition for one's contributions and efforts not only boosts morale but also cultivates a sense of purpose and accomplishment. This acknowledgment, whether through verbal appreciation, awards, or other forms of recognition, contributes to a positive work environment where individuals feel seen and respected. Positive well-being, in turn, extends beyond the professional sphere, influencing overall job satisfaction, motivation, and a sense of belonging within the organization. As employees experience a genuine sense of appreciation, their mental and emotional well-being is positively reinforced, creating a virtuous cycle that benefits both the individual and the workplace.

The Number One Thing That Employees Want from Their Managers

I won't beat around the bush: the number one thing that employees want from their managers is *care*. Now, care can take on many meanings. Care is a multifaceted concept that transcends its singular definition, encompassing various dimensions of human relationships and responsibilities. It embodies compassion, empathy, and consideration for others' well-being. Care involves a commitment to nurturing, protecting, and fostering growth. In the broader context, care extends to environmental stewardship and social responsibility, emphasizing the interconnectedness of humanity and the world. Ultimately, care is a dynamic and evolving expression of kindness and responsibility that manifests uniquely across diverse relationships and contexts, shaping the fabric of our personal and collective experiences. Care in the workplace is multifaceted as well: care to know what matters to me, care to speak my name in a room of opportunities that I'm not in, care to set boundaries, care to set expectations. So many use cases for care in the workplace.

Michael Scott from the TV show *The Office* is often regarded as the world's best boss (he has the mug to prove it) because he genuinely cares about his employees. Despite his quirks and bumbling idiocy, and 100 percent offensive yet not malicious nature, his caring qualities shine through, endearing him to both the characters in the show and the audience.[24] Let's examine the ways that Michael shows his care:

- **Personal interest:** Michael takes a keen interest in the lives of his employees, not just their work-related matters. He makes an effort to know about their hobbies, families, and personal struggles, demonstrating that he sees them as individuals beyond their roles in the office.

- **Supportive nature:** When employees face challenges or personal difficulties, Michael is there to offer support and encouragement. He creates an open environment where employees feel comfortable discussing their issues, knowing that he will lend a listening ear.

- **Celebrating milestones:** Michael celebrates the successes and milestones of his employees, both big and small. He takes pride in their accomplishments and ensures that their efforts are recognized and appreciated.

- **Team-building activities:** Michael goes to great lengths to organize team-building activities and events, aiming to foster a sense of camaraderie among his staff. He believes that strong team dynamics contribute to a more enjoyable and productive work environment.

- **Taking responsibility:** When he makes mistakes as a manager, Michael takes ownership of them. He may not always get it right, but he is willing to learn from his errors and make amends.

- **Creating a fun work environment:** Michael strives to inject humor and light-heartedness into the workplace. He believes that a fun and positive atmosphere can boost employee morale and make work more enjoyable.

- **Empathy and emotional connection:** Michael's caring nature comes through in moments of emotional connection with his employees. He shows empathy and compassion, trying to understand and support their feelings.

- **Going above and beyond:** Michael often goes above and beyond his managerial duties to help his employees. He puts in extra effort to make their lives better, even if it means sacrificing his comfort as a leader.

- **Standing up for his team:** When faced with challenges from upper management or outsiders, Michael defends his team fiercely. He values their contributions and stands up for their worth as individuals and professionals.

- **Embracing inclusion:** Michael encourages an inclusive atmosphere (okay, Toby Flenderson may not feel this way). He appreciates the unique talents and perspectives that each employee brings to the team.

Despite his flaws and occasional missteps, Michael Scott's caring nature sets him apart as a manager who truly values his employees. His dedication to building meaningful relationships and creating a supportive work environment makes him a *hard-to-forget* character in the world of television managers. That's what she said.

What's the Impact of Not Being Like Mike? What Happens When Leaders Don't Care?

Listen, we all know that bad leadership can have a profound impact on the workplace, creating a toxic work culture within an organization. At worst, when managers directly express a lack of care for their employees. More commonly, when leaders exhibit behaviors such as micromanagement, lack of transparency, favoritism, or failure to address conflicts, it can erode trust, communication, and morale among employees. And when leaders neglect their employees, it can have a profound and detrimental impact on their mental well-being. Employees who feel neglected by their leaders may experience feelings of worthlessness, disconnection, and isolation, leading to increased levels of stress, anxiety, and depression. The lack of support, recognition, and feedback from leaders can erode employees' confidence, motivation, and sense of belonging within the organization. This neglect can also contribute to a toxic work environment characterized by low morale, distrust, and poor communication, further exacerbating mental health issues among employees.

Studies have shown that employees who experience this lack of care from leader toxicity are more likely to suffer from chronic stress, anxiety, depression, and burnout. Ultimately, leaders' neglect of their employees' well-being not only undermines individual mental health but also hinders organizational success by impairing productivity, engagement, and retention. Putting it into dollars and cents, workplace stress is estimated to cost US businesses up to $300 billion annually in lost productivity, absenteeism, and healthcare expenses, according to research from the American Institute of Stress.[25] Additionally, the World Health Organization reports that work-related stress contributes to numerous health issues, including cardiovascular diseases, musculoskeletal disorders, and impaired immune function.[26] These statistics underscore the critical need for organizations to address bad leadership and toxic work cultures to protect the well-being and health of their employees.

In any situation in life, there will be people you don't like. Same goes for leaders and their employees. We all don't have to like each other, but we need to have some degree of care to coexist in a healthy manner. Do leaders need to be genuine in their care for their employees for employees to feel a sense of belonging at work? I mean, they can't all be like Mike (he legit cares). Truthfully, I could make an argument either way, but I've concluded that yes, leaders need to be genuine in their care for their employees in order for employees to feel a sense of belonging at work. Genuine care involves showing empathy, understanding, and respect for employees' well-being and individual needs. When leaders authentically demonstrate care and concern for their employees, it fosters trust, loyalty, and a positive work environment where employees feel valued, supported, and appreciated. This genuine care creates a sense of belonging by validating employees' experiences, fostering meaningful connections, and promoting a culture of inclusivity and mutual respect.

In contrast, leaders who exhibit insincerity or superficiality in their care for employees may create distrust, cynicism, and disengagement, undermining efforts to cultivate a sense of belonging within the organization. Authenticity in leadership is crucial for creating a workplace where employees feel a genuine sense of belonging and are motivated to contribute their best work. Do some leaders fake it? Do they pretend to care? Yes. Some leaders that fake it typically fake it in the interest of the bottom lines of productivity and job security. Make no mistake about it— the job security in this case is theirs and theirs only.

Does that make a leader who doesn't care or who cares more about themselves than their employees a narcissist? Nope. It's essential to distinguish between behaviors associated with narcissism and those associated with a lack of care or self- centeredness in leadership. While narcissistic traits may manifest in leaders who prioritize their needs and interests over those of their employees, not all leaders who exhibit self-centered behavior are narcissists. This distinction is important because labeling all self-centered leaders as narcissists oversimplifies complex behaviors and ignores other potential factors, such as stress or lack of self-awareness, that may influence their actions.

Part of Care Is Knowing

Knowing can go in so many directions...where to begin? Knowing is closely related to caring in the context of leadership as it reflects a leader's commitment to understanding and empathizing with their employees' needs, concerns, and experiences. Embracing knowledge and understanding in the workplace is essential for leaders as it enables them to make informed decisions, foster innovation, and effectively guide their teams toward success... and feel like the leader that they want to be, coaching and growing their people. The range of knowing is huge and I would never assume to capture it all, but here are some of the biggies. Let the knowing begin.

- **Knowing #1—know how to meet employees where they are.** To effectively meet employees where they are, it's essential to understand their unique needs, preferences, and challenges. This includes recognizing individual motivations, communication styles, and work environment considerations. Creating open feedback mechanisms, offering development opportunities tailored to their interests and skills, providing flexibility and support, and consistently showing appreciation for their contributions are crucial aspects of meeting employees where they are. In most cases, caring for employees and meeting them where they are means that managers need to know what their employees are experiencing outside of work as well. Understanding what employees are experiencing outside of work is crucial for manager care. This increased level of care enhances employees' sense of belonging by validating their individual experiences and fostering a stronger connection between personal well-being and professional life within the workplace. When employees don't feel this, they leave companies. For example, a participant from my research, let's call her Lisa, told me about an experience with her manager and how his lack of care prompted her to leave the company.

"And I remember saying something and he said, you know, [Lisa], I don't know your kids' names. And I really don't need to, nor do I want to. And I was like, I'm done. This is not right. You don't care about my kids' names. You'll never remember them, but you don't say that to me."

Lisa quit and other employees will also when managers can't and don't meet employees where they are.

- **Knowing #2—know that positioning yourself as a family (even when the culture promotes it) is a dangerous endeavor.** Companies use this as a flex, promoting the feeling of family in culture to promote connection. You are seen as the head of the family, the most influential person in the workplace, hands down. In this case, managers are seen

as mom and dad (as you already know) and the concept of
family heightened. If you are part of a culture where this is
the case, you need to know that familism introduces a host
of issues that outweigh positive aspirations. Employees
who consider their workplace to have a more familial
atmosphere reported feeling more betrayed when breaches
of trust occurred compared to those who perceived the
workplace as less familial. It's like that saying, "Don't let your
mouth write a check you can't cash." Perfection in familism
does not exist and yet, we search for the perfect family for
most of our lives. I cannot tell you how many stories about
hurt feelings and issues I've heard because employees are
searching for this perfect image of family at work. Managers
are not equipped to manage the psychological issues that
come with workplace parenting, and they face performance
issues when companies pursue familism. Remember, also,
that what family means to employees varies per individual,
per team, per culture—the delta is simply too large. That
coupled with mismatches between the promises made by
the company versus how they are or are not actualized by
the company is a recipe for uncertainty and ambiguity, with
managers left holding the bag. Research shows that the
concept of familism causes a host of problems for managers
left to reset expectations when familism damages an
employee's mental state and causes problems for them.

- **Knowing #3—Know that your words matter.** The word
  family is an obvious trigger (and red flag). The words that a
  manager chooses when communicating with an employee
  hold immense importance, shaping the employee's
  perception of their role, contribution, and value within the
  organization. Hold up—actually, they do more than that—
  they shape how the employee sees themselves as a person:
  their identity. So, words matter beyond the workplace and
  workday. Effective communication from a manager can

inspire, motivate, and empower employees by providing clear direction, meaningful feedback, and recognition for their efforts. Positive and encouraging words from a manager can boost morale, foster a sense of belonging, and strengthen the employee-manager relationship, leading to increased engagement, productivity, job satisfaction, and happiness. Conversely, negative or careless words can have a detrimental impact, eroding trust, damaging morale, and hindering performance. Toxic and negative conversations spill over outside of the workplace—they can disrupt our sleep patterns, give us stress, and derail after-work hours by way of situations we experience. Therefore, the choice of words from a manager to an employee is critical. We will dive deeper into language in the next chapter, promise.

- **Knowing #4—Know how hard it is to speak truth to power.** This is hard at all levels. This isn't so much of a reach since we all have a person above us in the workplace (even CEOs have boards to report to). Speaking truth to power at work can be challenging for several reasons. There may be a fear of consequences or retaliation, especially if the truth challenges established norms, practices, or decisions made by those in positions of authority. We all may worry about negative repercussions such as being marginalized, ostracized, or even facing disciplinary action for speaking up—and work is tied to our livelihood, so the stakes are high. Additionally, power dynamics within organizations can create barriers to honest communication, as employees may feel intimidated or powerless when addressing issues with higher-ranking individuals. If you are a leader, recognize how hard this is. You have the same upward challenges. Think about it—there can be a culture of silence or conformity in some workplaces, where speaking out against the status quo is discouraged or viewed negatively. This can result in individuals hesitating to voice their concerns or offer dissenting opinions, even when they believe it is in their own or the organization's best interest. Are you providing a mechanism or channel for constructive feedback and open dialogue? If not, it can make it even more challenging for employees to express their perspectives and raise important issues without fear of backlash.

- **Knowing #5—Know how important it is to give employees the space to process, but don't leave them alone too long.** Leaders need to give their employees space to process as a form of caring, recognizing that individuals may need time and privacy to reflect, digest information, and make sense of their in-and-out-of-the-workplace experiences. This space allows employees to process their thoughts and emotions, leading to more thoughtful and informed decision-making, improved problem-solving, and a greater sense of autonomy and empowerment. By respecting employees' need for space and providing support without being intrusive, leaders demonstrate empathy, trust, and understanding, fostering a positive work environment where employees feel valued, heard, and respected. Be there for them, check in, and remember that too much space may feel like neglect.

For example, in my research, a participant (let's call her Mindy) told me about a time when it felt like her world came crashing down. Her father was ill. Mindy let her manager know, and one month later her dad's health got progressively worse. Her manager knew all of this, but she never asked Mindy how she was doing. She never asked Mindy how her dad was doing. She never offered Mindy more time off to be with him or the option of remote work to spend time with her dad. Mindy's dad died a few weeks later. She was allowed five days of unpaid leave to bury him, but started receiving calls asking when she would return before those five days were up. Reflecting on that time, Mindy said that she traded in spending the last weeks of her dad's life with him and her mental health for a tortuous and toxic job. She was not given the time and permission to process—and that care from her manager would have gone a long way.

- **Knowing #6—Know that employees take past managers with them from job to job.** That's right. If you are a manager, please know that you are not the only manager present with employees who report to you. No, I'm not talking about your manager, upline, or even peer-adjacent managers. When we think of the role that managers play in an employee's sense of belonging at work, it's important to know that past managers need to be factored into the equation. In fact, **we carry up to three managers from our past into every new manager relationship we take on.** Why is that? Well. When it's good with a manager, we hold future managers to that bar, and when it's bad, it can take years to recover fully from a toxic manager. In my research on traumatic belonging experiences related to prior managers, employees told me that unless they sought outside help or support, their traumatic sense of belonging went unresolved with lasting physical, physiological, and psychological effects that could take anywhere from one to ten years to resolve. When manager-related trauma is left unresolved, shame and uncertainty are amplified, ultimately undermining an individual's sense of belonging and limiting the ability to achieve full self-actualization—all fun to bring into a new work environment, right? Conversely, when employees experience a positive experience with their manager, it can result in a positive sense of belonging. It serves as the blueprint for how they want to interact with future managers. Knowing the overall impact that past managers have had on your current employees is a must. Remember, it varies greatly, with the effects being long-lasting, so a great question around this may be, "What did you like about past managers and what didn't you like?"

Can you think of three (or more) managers from your past? Chart them out on this axis.

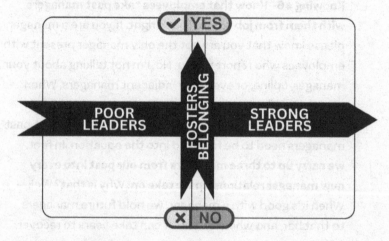

How many of the strong managers you listed fostered belonging for you? And the poor ones?

In the next chapter, we will take on some of what you are figuring out to see how you get alignment at work—or if it's time for you to move on.

A toxic relationship with a bad manager can have profound neurological impacts, affecting key brain regions such as the amygdala, prefrontal cortex, and the body's stress response system. Continuous stress and negative interactions can lead to hyperactivity in the amygdala, heightening emotional responses and feelings of fear and anxiety. Prolonged exposure to stress hormones like cortisol can impair the prefrontal cortex's function, affecting decision-making and emotional regulation. Additionally, dysregulation of the stress response system can lead to imbalances in cortisol levels, impacting physical health, mood, and cognitive abilities. The neurological impacts of a toxic relationship with a bad manager messes with an individual's sense of belonging in the workplace and beyond. When employees experience chronic stress and emotional distress due to a toxic relationship, it can undermine their sense of safety, trust, and connection within the organization. This can contribute to feelings of isolation, alienation, and a lack of belonging, as employees may struggle to form meaningful relationships and engage with their work in a positive and fulfilling way. And if only we could leave it behind when we "leave work" for the day.

Want an example? Let's go trauma bonding. Trauma bonding occurs when an individual forms a psychological and emotional attachment to their abuser through a cycle of positive reinforcement. In the workplace, one of the most common examples of trauma bonding occurs in an abusive manager-employee relationship, typically with the development of a powerful emotional connection forged through shared adversity, typically characterized by the manager's harmful behavior and the employee's vulnerability. This toxic dynamic often arises from the misuse of power, with the manager exerting control, employing manipulation tactics such as gaslighting, and creating an environment of fear and dependency. The cycle of abuse, marked by periods of mistreatment interspersed with seemingly supportive gestures, contributes to the employee's difficulty in breaking away. The victim may endure isolation, threats, and a decline in self-esteem, fostering a sense of attachment that makes it challenging to recognize and escape the damaging nature of the relationship. Taking it even further, trauma bonding can have significant neurological impacts, activating brain regions associated with attachment and reward, such as the amygdala and the release of dopamine. This is why the toxic bond can create a powerful emotional attachment to the person causing harm, despite the negative consequences, leading to difficulties in breaking free from the toxic relationship, and once they break free from the relationship with the abuser, they can also experience manager PTSD for years to follow.

How Can Managers Identify and Care For Their Employees Experiencing Each of the Four Types of Belonging?

Managers can best identify and care for employees with **true belonging** by being genuinely curious about their team members' experiences and regularly engaging in heartfelt one-on-one conversations. Look for signs of enthusiasm, active participation, and strong, positive relationships, as these are indicators of true belonging. While managing an employee with true belonging is much easier than the inverse, don't take your foot off the pedal because true belonging still comes with challenges for you to watch for, including navigating diverse perspectives. True belonging involves embracing diverse perspectives and backgrounds, but individuals with a strong sense of belonging may still need your help to navigate and appreciate differing viewpoints, balance their experiences with those of others, and foster inclusive dialogue. You want to make sure they honor different backgrounds and experiences, fostering a rich, inclusive dialogue and not just voicing their own. To avoid groupthink, encourage innovation and diverse viewpoints.

Also, conflicts arise even in cohesive environments, necessitating respectful communication and common ground. Balancing personal and professional boundaries ensures we don't lose ourselves to our work, maintaining our well-being while contributing meaningfully to our community. Individuals with true belonging may face the challenge of effectively managing conflicts that may arise between colleagues with different opinions, values, or approaches. Maintaining respectful communication and finding common ground can be crucial in such situations. Individuals with true belonging may find themselves in a position to be allies and advocates for colleagues still striving for a sense of belonging. Encourage them to actively support and amplify the voices of marginalized individuals, challenge exclusionary practices, and promote diversity and inclusion.

When managers are faced with employees who are experiencing *thwarted belonging*, they need to take a compassionate, proactive approach to recognize and address these feelings. It starts with being attuned to subtle changes in behavior—like withdrawal from team activities, minimal communication, and a noticeable dip in productivity or enthusiasm. Managers should engage in open, empathetic conversations to understand the underlying causes, validating the employee's feelings without judgment. By fostering a supportive environment where employees feel seen, heard, and valued and by implementing personalized strategies to reconnect them with the team, managers can help restore their sense of belonging, enhancing both individual well-being and overall team cohesion.

Managers can best identify employees with a *sacrificial belonging* by paying close attention to signs of overwork, stress, and reluctance to voice personal views and challenges. Regular one-on-one check-ins that encourage open and honest communication can reveal if employees feel they must compromise their personal values or well-being to fit in. Look for behavioral cues like consistently working late, avoiding conflict, or showing signs of burnout. Managers can best care for employees with a sacrificial sense of belonging by actively fostering a supportive and balanced work environment, embracing empathy with heart. Okay, I don't mean bleeding heart; I am not getting sappy on you all. This means recognizing the signs of burnout and overwork, and creating a culture where employees feel seen and valued for who they truly are, not for their output. Managers should recognize and address this by setting clear boundaries and providing support like that given to endurance athletes by their coaches, protecting employees from the erosion of self and preventing burnout. Encourage boundaries and self-care and celebrate authenticity over conformity. Acknowledge and value the efforts of employees, while also promoting self-care and ensuring the sacrifices made are not at a personal expense.

Managers, listen up: identifying and caring for employees with *dissimulated belonging* isn't just about recognizing the obvious signs of disconnection; it's about tuning into the nuances of human behavior. It is perfectly fine for people not to want to be corporate cheerleaders, for them to have or want to find most or all of their fulfillment from their life outside of the office. Remember, they are still team players. Make sure not to type-cast them as slackers because they may lack connection to the culture. They should not be seen as less productive or not caring about their job, disconnected from, and apathetic to, the workplace environment and the people around them. Employees with dissimulated belonging struggle. They have a real fear of being judged or misunderstood which can hinder their ability to openly contribute and participate in team projects. Be mindful that these employees often wear masks, conforming outwardly while feeling deeply disconnected inside. Look for signs of excessive conformity, avoidance of genuine interaction, or mimicking colleagues' behaviors to fit in. The key here is vulnerability. Create a safe space for authentic conversations where trust is built, not assumed. Show empathy, ask open-ended questions, and listen without judgment. By fostering a culture of genuine connection and psychological safety, you invite dissimulated employees to bring their true selves to work, dismantling the façade and nurturing a real sense of belonging.

Leave People Better Than You Found Them

The goal is simple: leave people better than you found them. The truth is that people leave when managers don't care, and their sense of belonging takes a major hit. Should good leadership and care be advanced common sense for managers? If that is the case, why have managers veered so far from this? Or have they? If so, why aren't employees telling them? It is hard, hard, hard for employees to speak truth to power. It's not a level playing field. Managers and their employees are not equals and it is important that the manager recognizes the emotional impact they have on their subordinates, that they are mindful of unintended consequences.

A manager's role encompasses not just overseeing tasks but also nurturing the growth, well-being, and sense of belonging of their subordinates. From the moment we first connect to our journey of development inside of a company, we earn the trust of each person we work with, but the magic is when we aren't in front of them, they feel they belong, have purpose and are important to the larger cause. As leaders, managers are expected to shepherd their employees through this experience providing empathy and support and open and honest communication.

When managers actively invest in their employees' success and development, they not only enhance individual performance but also cultivate a sense of belonging by demonstrating care, respect, and a genuine interest in their team members' professional and personal advancement.

Chapter 6
Getting Aligned on Workplace Belonging

Once we have donned our Sorting Hat and been appointed to the metaphorical house of Hogwarts we are casting our lot with, then what? At the end of this belongingness journey in the workforce, we must consider more than just where we've landed. People come into the workplace with implicit values. When I am hired, it reaffirms that I have value. They join a company because they believe it shares similar values to their own. This chapter discusses the fallout that occurs when the values of the workplace are misaligned (like being a Slytherin in Hufflepuff's common room) with your personally held values, misalignment in general and how it impacts your sense of belonging.[27]

Everyone Belongs Here

Does everyone belong? It sure feels like companies are making that push with all of the "belonging" weeks taking place. Many of them with the super creative title "Belonging Week" with even more creative catchphrases like, "You belong here." When companies impose a statement that "everyone belongs" without fostering a genuine culture of inclusion and when belonging is pushed rather than chosen, it can lead to a dangerous form of imposed belonging. Imposed belonging occurs when an organization enforces conformity, making employees feel pressured to fit in. Imposed belonging can lead to several negative outcomes, including stress, reduced job satisfaction, and burnout, as individuals struggle to maintain a façade. Unlike true belonging, where acceptance and inclusion are based on genuine connections and shared values, imposed belonging is characterized by a superficial sense of inclusion that can be detrimental to both the individual and the organization. True belonging must be earned through genuine practices and experiences.

Imposed belonging creates pressure for employees to conform and mask their true selves to fit the company's ideal, leading to inauthentic interactions and increased stress—and secrecy. No one wants to go against the grain on this stuff; it feels bad. Employees may feel that they must hide aspects of their identity to avoid standing out, which can result in feelings of isolation and emotional exhaustion. Over time, this enforced conformity can erode trust, stifle creativity, and hinder open communication, ultimately damaging both employee well-being and organizational health.

In situations of imposed belonging, individuals feel pressured to conform to a group or organizational norms and values to be accepted. This type of belonging is not naturally developed but is instead forced upon individuals, often leading to a sense of disconnection and inauthenticity. People may feel that they have to hide their true selves or adopt behaviors and attitudes that do not align with their personal values to fit in and be part of the group.

How Do Our Values Shape Us and Our Sense of Belonging?

Our individual traits and values contribute to our sense of belonging and the way we make sense of the world. Belonging is essentially an individual's perception (no one else can decide it for you, that's inclusion) of themselves and how they feel connected in a particular context—whether the setting is within self, or outside of self. Looking at belonging at the individual level requires looking through the lens of how an individual makes sense of their belonging. It also warrants examining how self-perceptions of identity, traits, and personal values shape an individual's sense of belonging.

Personal values influence sensemaking, and the outcomes of an individual's sensemaking become their perception and judgment. Walton and Brady posited that belonging is fundamentally the perception of fit between an individual's self and their setting.[28] Thus, personal values are an essential source that informs a sense of belonging.

Just How Important Are Values in the Workplace?

Values are the heartbeat of any workplace, shaping everything from motivation to decision-making and job satisfaction. When our personal values align with those of our organization, we feel a deeper sense of belonging. This alignment allows us to bring our whole selves to work, fostering an environment where we can thrive and contribute meaningfully. On the other hand, when there's a misalignment between personal and organizational values, it creates a sense of disconnection and alienation. Organizations that understand and nurture this alignment help cultivate a culture of trust and engagement, where employees feel they truly belong without compromising who they are.

Values in the workplace are the guiding principles that influence how employees are expected to think, act, and feel on the job. They are the compass that helps individuals navigate their work life with a sense of purpose and alignment. For example, if a company values transparency, it will prioritize open communication, where employees are encouraged to share their ideas and concerns without fear of reprisal. At times, the positive values like transparency teach employees things they didn't know they needed. Values are not just a game of companies catching up; companies can also create a culture where values like transparency promote growth and kindness! This not only builds trust but also fosters a culture where employees feel valued, understood, and cared for, enhancing their sense of belonging and engagement. When employees' personal values align with these organizational values, they are more likely to feel fulfilled and motivated, contributing to a positive and productive work environment.

When our personal values resonate with those of our organization, it fosters a sense of belonging and fulfillment. This connection between personal and organizational values is crucial because it means we're not just clocking in and out for a paycheck; we're part of something bigger that aligns with who we are at our core. This alignment empowers us to show up authentically, driving engagement, satisfaction, and a deep sense of community in the workplace.

Understanding how we index our personal values and compare them with workplace values involves a complex interplay of cognitive and emotional processes. From a neurological perspective, our brains are wired to seek alignment between personal values and those of our workplace to reduce cognitive dissonance (the mental discomfort experienced when holding two conflicting beliefs, values, or attitudes at the same time) and enhance psychological comfort. Employees constantly evaluate whether their personal values align with those of their organization by reflecting on their daily experiences and interactions. When we see our values reflected in our company's mission and actions, it lights up our brain's reward system, boosting our feelings of satisfaction, motivation, belonging, and overall well-being. On a practical level, this means employees observe the company's actions, culture, and leadership behaviors to determine if they match their core values, such as integrity, respect, and community involvement. When there is a clear alignment, it reduces cognitive dissonance and enhances overall well-being, allowing employees to show up authentically and fully engage in their work. This alignment engages the prefrontal cortex, which is responsible for complex decision-making and social behaviors, reinforcing a sense of belonging and purpose within the organization. In essence, when our values and our work align, we feel more connected, authentic, and fulfilled.

Sometimes a company's values may resonate with us and become aspirational. For example, you may already believe in philanthropy and consider it important to you, but it may become more of a priority based on the way a company lives its values. When a company champions corporate philanthropy, it often resonates deeply with employees whose personal values align with giving back to the community. An employee might be inspired to join and stay with a company because of its robust corporate social responsibility programs. They see the company not only as a place to work but as a vehicle for making a positive impact in the world. This alignment transforms their work from just a job into a mission, creating a sense of purpose and belonging that is both personal and aspirational. Employees who align with a company's commitment to social responsibility and community service may feel a greater sense of fulfillment and pride in their work. When personal values align with the values of an organization, something powerful happens. It doesn't just reduce stress; it deepens job satisfaction and creates a genuine sense of belonging. Employees start to feel that their work is about more than just business goals—it's contributing to something meaningful, something that resonates on a personal level.

What Happens When Personal Values and Work Values Don't Align at Work?

People find real meaning when they can connect their time and effort to the values that matter most to them. When personal values and work values don't align, it can create a profound sense of dissonance and unease. When we join a company, we hope that our core beliefs and principles will be reflected in our daily work. But when these expectations clash with reality, we find ourselves in a constant state of internal conflict. We start questioning our role and place within the organization, leading to feelings of isolation and disconnection. When our values don't line up with our work, it's not just a "job thing"—it seeps into our personal well-being, fueling stress and anxiety.

Imagine showing up to work every day knowing that your fundamental values, like integrity or respect, are not mirrored by your company's actions. It's like trying to fit a square peg into a round hole. You might begin to feel like an imposter, pretending to support initiatives or decisions that go against your core beliefs just to avoid rocking the boat. This kind of environment stifles authentic self-expression and forces you to wear a mask, hiding your true self from your colleagues and leaders. Over time, this erodes your sense of identity and belonging, making you feel like an outsider in your workplace.

The impact of this misalignment extends beyond emotional well-being. It can also undermine professional relationships and career progression. When employees speak up about these misalignments, they risk being labeled as nonconformists or troublemakers. In my research, many employees told me that they would rather stay quiet than stand up for themselves and voice their concerns about value misalignment only to face repercussions, such as damaged relationships with managers or being overlooked for promotions. This not only hinders their career growth but also reinforces a culture of silence and conformity, where employees feel pressured to suppress their true selves to fit in.

The consequences of misaligned values are not just personal; they ripple through the organization, affecting overall morale and productivity. Employees who feel disconnected from their company's values are less likely to be engaged or motivated. They may perform their tasks without passion or commitment, leading to a decline in the quality of work and innovation. In contrast, when personal and organizational values align, it creates a powerful synergy that drives engagement, fosters a deep sense of belonging, and enhances overall well-being. Therefore, it's crucial for companies to genuinely understand and integrate the diverse values of their employees to build a thriving, inclusive workplace.

Failure to adhere to an organization's values and norms may put tremendous stress on employees. Cue the duck syndrome—on the surface, everything might look calm and composed, but underneath, employees are paddling furiously, struggling to keep up appearances while dealing with the internal turmoil caused by this value clash. Employees, desperate to fit in and avoid the repercussions of misalignment, put on a façade of competence and satisfaction, all the while feeling disconnected and disheartened inside. The process of covering this misalignment takes a toll. Employees might overcompensate by working longer hours, taking on more responsibilities, or excessively conforming to workplace norms to seem like they belong. They become actors in their lives, performing a role that doesn't reflect their identity, which only deepens their sense of isolation and disconnection. It's a painful cycle that not only affects their professional lives but also seeps into their personal lives, impacting their mental health and overall happiness.

When your values don't line up with what's happening at work, listen up—this isn't just something that affects you from 9 to 5. It's there when you walk in the door at night, it's there at dinner with your family, and it's there when you're lying awake, wondering why you're exhausted. That misalignment? It eats at you because every day, you're stuck pretending to be someone you're not. And that constant internal conflict is draining. It's why you're snapping at your loved ones or zoning out when they're talking—it's hard to be present when you're carrying around a mountain of stress and frustration from work. Here's the truth: the longer you ignore this disconnect, the harder it's going to be to bring your true self anywhere, let alone your personal life. You owe it to yourself and to the people who matter most to close the gap between who you are and who you're pretending to be. Because trust me, that gap is where real happiness starts slipping away.

When our values don't line up with what we're doing at work, it doesn't just frustrate us—it starts to chip away at our self-worth. Spending so much time in a place where we can't show up as ourselves? Before you know it, you're questioning your own integrity and worthiness. That's when self-doubt, insecurity, and even shame creep in. It's tough to pursue our own goals or feel joy outside of work when we're in a constant battle with ourselves. And this isn't just about career satisfaction—it's about living fully. The truth is, misaligned values don't just drain our energy; they rob us of the meaningful life we all deserve. This isn't just about work; it's about reclaiming your worth.

The Hidden Wounds: Navigating Value Rejection and Misalignment in the Workplace

Disagreeing with a norm or value in the workplace can be challenging. It may sometimes lead to feelings of social disconnection, which can affect an individual's sense of belonging in the workplace. When we stand up for our values and face rejection, it feels like a personal attack on who we are at our core. This kind of social rejection isn't just uncomfortable—it's profoundly painful. It triggers a visceral response that taps into our deepest fears of not being good enough or not belonging. This can significantly damage our perception of belonging in the workplace, leaving us feeling isolated and undervalued. It's like reliving past traumas where our worthiness was questioned, and our need for connection was unmet. This kind of rejection not only affects our professional identity but also resonates with old wounds, amplifying our sense of pain and disconnection. It's a stark reminder that belonging isn't just about being included; it's about being accepted and valued for who we truly are—both by others and by ourselves. When our values are dismissed, it feels like a rejection of our essence, making it challenging to feel safe and connected in the workplace.

In addition, there is a profound connection between cognitive processes, rejection, and trauma, particularly in the workplace. Working memory, our brain's ability to hold and manipulate information over short periods, is crucial for tasks like problem-solving and decision-making. When employees face misalignment between their personal values and their workplace environment, their working memory is tasked with constantly reconciling this dissonance. This ongoing process is not only mentally exhausting but can also lead to cognitive overload. Think of it like a computer running too many programs at once—eventually, it slows down or crashes.

One more analogy: imagine your working memory as a small whiteboard where you jot down important notes. When your values and the company's actions are in conflict, it's like trying to fit too much information on this whiteboard—it quickly becomes cluttered, ineffective, and smeared. This overload is like the cognitive strain experienced during traumatic events, where the mind struggles to process and make sense of overwhelming information.

Rejection in the workplace compounds this issue. When we feel rejected or dismissed because our values don't align with those of our organization, it's not just a simple letdown—it's a direct hit to our sense of self-worth and belonging. This rejection can trigger trauma responses, activating the same areas of the brain involved in processing physical pain. Over time, the constant need to navigate and reconcile these experiences of rejection can drain our working memory capacity and exacerbate feelings of stress and anxiety.

But wait, there's more. The hidden wounds from misalignment and rejection can have a lasting impact long after you shut your laptop to end the workday. Prolonged cognitive strain can result in cognitive fatigue, reducing the brain's ability to process information effectively. This leads to difficulties in concentration, problem-solving, and decision-making, making everyday tasks increasingly challenging. Additionally, persistent mental overload is closely linked to heightened stress and anxiety levels, which can evolve into serious mental health conditions such as depression and anxiety disorders.

The impact of cognitive overload reaches far beyond just mental health—it spills over into our social connections and even our physical well-being. When our minds are overwhelmed, it becomes harder to fully engage in meaningful interactions, and we might start to pull back from social activities. This withdrawal can lead to feelings of isolation and put a strain on our relationships with friends, family, and colleagues. Over time, the stress and strain make it harder to focus, slowing us down and even stifling our creativity. Physically, the effects are real too: chronic stress from mental overload can show up as headaches, high blood pressure, digestive issues, and a weakened immune system.

How Can You Brave the Workplace When You Are at a Values Impasse?

When you find yourself at an impasse where your values don't align with your workplace and leaving isn't an option due to livelihood concerns, bravery means finding ways to navigate this difficult terrain with resilience and resourcefulness. First, anchor yourself in your core values and use them as your guiding star. After all, the more you fall back on sacrificing what makes you, you, it's not fostering belonging, it's just fitting in—and it is so common for employees to experience social pressure to fit in, adhere to corporate norms, and align to organizational values. Norms have an oppressing effect and are associated with social pressure that may lead people to conform.

So, how to make sure you don't lose yourself? Bravery! I know it's scary, it always is, but engage in open, respectful conversations with your supervisors and colleagues, expressing how certain practices or policies conflict with your values. Frame these discussions around potential benefits for the organization, such as increased trust and employee engagement, and propose constructive solutions that could bridge the gap between your values and the company's practices. This can create small but meaningful shifts in your work environment.

Meanwhile, focus on what you can control. Establish personal boundaries (don't worry, there are lots on boundaries coming up in Chapter 7) to protect your well-being and seek out aspects of your job that do resonate with your values, even if they are small. Look for projects, tasks, or initiatives where you can make a positive impact and find fulfillment. Build a support network of colleagues who share similar values or can empathize with your situation, providing you with emotional support and a sense of community. Practice self-care to maintain your mental and emotional resilience. Remember, bravery in this context is about navigating the tension with grace and integrity, finding ways to stay true to your values while managing the constraints of your situation. It's about taking small, courageous steps each day to ensure that you're making choices that honor who you are.

Other Types of Misalignments in the Workplace

Personality Misalignment

Individuals constantly evaluate who they are and where they belong, and this ongoing assessment is deeply influenced by their personality traits—the unique ways they think, feel, and connect with others. One of those traits, moral sensitivity, is that special trait that guides our decision-making through a lens of ethics and morality, helping us choose what's right based on our core values and principles. Moral sensitivity and agency relate to our sense of intentionality, perspective-taking, and sense-making. This is important because although people may experience the same thing at the same time, it is common for them to make sense of what they experience differently. Personality profoundly influences a person's experience and construct of belonging.

Personality traits like extraversion/introversion, agreeableness, and openness to experience are critical in shaping how we perceive and interact with our work environment. For example, individuals high in extraversion often seek out and thrive in social interactions, which can enhance their sense of belonging. Conversely, those lower in extraversion might find it challenging to connect, potentially feeling more isolated.

Meet Dean, a thoughtful and reserved teacher who recently joined a bustling school known for its dynamic, extroverted culture. From day one, Dean felt out of place. Faculty meetings were loud and fast-paced, dominated by a few confident voices. Dean, who valued deep reflection and careful consideration, found it difficult to participate in these conversations—it was too much stimulation and not enough time for digestion. In the classroom, Dean preferred to engage students through quiet, meaningful discussions and individualized attention, but the school culture prioritized energetic group activities and constant collaboration. Despite feeling uncomfortable, Dean tried to adapt by mimicking the behaviors of his more celebrated colleagues. He forced himself to speak up more often during staff meetings, adopting a louder and more assertive tone than felt natural. He participated in lively school events and social gatherings, even though it drained his energy. While this helped Dean fit in on the surface, it led to a heavy sense of disconnection, as if he was constantly wearing a mask to avoid judgment.

During curriculum planning sessions, Dean often deferred to the most dominant teachers in the room, fearing that his ideas would be dismissed or ridiculed. When his contributions were not met with support, Dean's confidence eroded further, making him believe his true self was neither valued nor accepted. Over time, this dissonance took a toll on Dean's mental health and sense of belonging. He felt increasingly isolated, believing he could never truly be himself in this environment. Dean's introverted nature, which once brought a unique perspective and creativity to his teaching methods, was overshadowed by the constant pressure to conform. Dean's story is a stark reminder of the importance of creating room for diverse personalities.

Now, meet Logan, a vibrant and outgoing senior civil engineer who recently joined a construction firm known for its calm, methodical culture. Logan was used to a fast-paced, louder construction site and wanted to try something new, but felt like a fish out of water from day one. The company's environment was marked by reserved and meticulous planning meetings, with lengthy

deliberations over every project detail. Logan, who excelled in
dynamic discussions and on-the-spot problem-solving, struggled
to connect with the introspective and more analytical aspects
of this construction site. Trying to adapt, Logan toned down
his energy, softened his voice during project discussions, and
slowed his pace to explain more to the less tenured engineers
on site. The people around him tended to observe and absorb
their surroundings quietly, processing experiences deeply before
expressing their thoughts and feelings. He wanted to be respectful
and learn from them, but the effort to adapt to this different style
left Logan feeling like he was wearing a mask, stifling his natural
energy and passion.

As time passed, this mismatch took a significant toll on Logan's
mental health and sense of belonging. He felt increasingly
alienated, unable to fully engage with his colleagues or the work
itself. Logan's extroverted nature, which once drove him to
lead collaborative efforts and innovate on-site solutions, was
overshadowed by the pressure to fit into the quieter, more solitary
work style of his peers and the vibe of the company in general. He
found himself holding back in meetings, hesitant to propose new
ideas or challenge existing plans, fearing his approach would be
seen as disruptive or like he was jumping the gun. It made Logan
question his career, if he was good at his job and he felt hopeless.

When employees like Dean and Logan are forced to hide their true
personalities, it not only affects their individual well-being but
also deprives the organization of the full range of their talents and
insights. This ongoing suppression of one's personality erodes
confidence and makes employees feel undervalued. Dean and
Logan's experiences around misalignment highlight the essential
need for workplaces to embrace diverse personality traits. The
pressure and struggle to conform is real. Time and time again in my
research, employees told me that they followed the opinions of

the most dominant person in their room and, furthermore, if they didn't feel that they could express their opinions safely, they felt like they could not be themselves. Additionally, study results also indicated a more general trend among introverted participants regarding not feeling as strong of a sense of belonging as others in their more extroverted company cultures and vice versa when more extroverted employees work for introverted companies/ leadership, and thus they don't feel they could be themselves as much. I heard hundreds of stories focused on personality and how accepted or not accepted it was by peers, management, and company culture. It made sense when employees reported feeling like they had to cover their identities to fit into their extroverted work environments.

In 2012, Susan Cain posited that workplaces are designed with extroverts in mind, favoring open floor plans, constant collaboration, and a fast-paced environment that can overwhelm introverts.[29] This setup often leaves introverted employees feeling out of place, as their need for quiet reflection and deep focus is overlooked. Conversely, when a company culture is primarily introverted, extroverted employees may struggle with the lack of dynamic interaction and spontaneous engagement, feeling stifled and disconnected. Susan Cain's work on personality faking shows that acting against one's natural tendencies can sometimes be necessary, but concealing one's true nature often leads to a deep sense of disconnection and fear of social judgment. Personality misalignment can erode confidence and engagement, ultimately impacting mental health and overall contribution to the organization...and for the record, I am team Jess (IYKYK).

Language Misalignment

Language is a powerful tool in the workplace, shaping interactions, perceptions, and the overall culture. Language can either foster a sense of belonging or create barriers that lead to disconnection and misunderstandings. When the language used by leaders and peers aligns with the values and identity of the employees, it can significantly enhance their sense of inclusion and belonging. Conversely, when there is a misalignment, it can lead to feelings of alienation and exclusion.

The language used in policies can either foster a sense of belonging or create barriers that lead to disconnection and misunderstandings. Clear, inclusive, thoughtful, and respectful language in policies ensures that employees feel valued and understood, which enhances their engagement and sense of belonging. On the other hand, ambiguous or insensitive language can lead to confusion, misinterpretation, and a toxic work environment where employees feel alienated and undervalued.

When the language in workplace policies does not align with the values and identities of the employees, it creates a significant gap that is hard to bridge. For instance, policies that use aggressive or competitive language or even outdated language can make employees feel out of place, unsupported, and undervalued. This misalignment can decrease engagement and productivity as employees struggle to align their personal values with the organizational culture. Employees might find themselves constantly second-guessing their words and actions, fearing misinterpretation or judgment, which can lead to a mentally exhausting environment and a diminished sense of belonging at best. Language misalignment is like trying to run a marathon in quicksand. You're constantly struggling to keep up, drained and frustrated, because everything feels out of sync with who you are and how you communicate. The mismatch kills your energy and focus, and before you know it, you're barely hanging on—let alone thriving. The feeling of belonging uncertainty may feel off the charts—the feeling of the end of the world versus the end of a long workday.

Perhaps even more than language in workplace policies, though, the language used by leaders and peers on a day-to-day basis can have a large unintended impact on employees' well-being and sense of belonging. For example, Meredith, a participant in one of my studies, opened up in one of our conversations about her struggle with mental health challenges and the impact of casual, thoughtless language in the workplace. She described how difficult it was to sit through meetings where colleagues tossed around terms like "bipolar," "psychotic," or "crazy" as jokes. Each time, it felt like a punch to the gut, a stark reminder that the environment wasn't safe for Meredith to be her true self. "They don't know how much of an insult that is," she said. "I don't feel included right then and there. It's like a spotlight on my differences, and not in a good way."

Meredith went on to explain how these moments of casual cruelty chipped away at her sense of belonging: "I can't always be myself; people would judge me, and I would have to relive something that can feel pretty bad. I don't want that stigma following me around in the office." Her story is a powerful reminder that the words we use matter deeply. Workplace language that includes casual, derogatory terms or insensitive jokes can undermine an individual's sense of belonging by highlighting their differences and creating a hostile environment. Words can either build bridges of understanding and connection or erect walls of exclusion, hurt, and thwarted belonging.

Workplace vernacular and phrases can contribute to a toxic environment, significantly impacting employees' sense of belonging and well-being. Mottos and phrases like "can't stop, won't stop" can contribute to a toxic environment, significantly impacting employees' sense of belonging and well-being (sorry Swifties).[30] While intended to promote perseverance and dedication, such mottos can inadvertently pressure employees to overwork and ignore their personal limits, leading to burnout and stress. When language used in the workplace doesn't align with employees' needs for balance and support, it fosters a culture where individuals feel they must constantly push themselves to the brink to be valued. This relentless drive can make employees feel undervalued and expendable, eroding their sense of belonging and overall mental health...and all from a motto that probably seemed innocent and inspirational to a leadership team.

The long-term impact of misaligned language in the workplace is profound. It can erode trust between employees and leadership, as the inconsistency between spoken values and the actual language used becomes more apparent. True story: my friend Suki had a manager who once called her a character assassin and she almost died right then and there. She was mortified and immediately apologetic. After a little time away from the situation, Suki asked her manager for examples of why she had said that, and she had the nerve to say to Suki, "That's not important." WTH? Of course it was important. Suki started to believe that maybe she was 007, killing people's credibility. She was sick over this and over time, started to disengage, feeling that she was no longer right for the organization. This disengagement was not just a personal setback but also a significant loss for the organization, as it wasn't able to tap into Suki's full potential. About a month afterward, she asked again about examples, and her manager asked me why she was being so persistent about this. She couldn't remember why Suki was asking to begin with, and Suki reminded her that she said

Suki was becoming a character assassin to which she said, "Suki, stop being so dramatic. I meant that you needed to stop talking shit, not that you were ruining people's careers." *Whoa.* If she had told Suki that originally, her reaction would have been different; it's a lot easier to focus on stopping one behavior (though, like Suki, I would have still needed examples!) than to hear yourself labeled as a specific negative kind of person. Language matters so much because it can profoundly impact our self-perception and how we are perceived by others. In Suki's case, being labeled a "character assassin" eroded her confidence and made her question her actions, leading to disengagement and a sense of not belonging in the organization.

Misalignment Is Trauma and It Fucks Us Up

Misalignment in the workplace is more than just a minor inconvenience; it's a form of trauma that deeply affects us. When our values, needs, and communication styles don't align with those of our organization, it creates a constant state of tension and stress. This misalignment disrupts our sense of belonging, making us feel out of place and undervalued. This ongoing conflict can lead to emotional exhaustion, anxiety, and a diminished sense of self-worth. When we can't be ourselves and we feel disconnected from our work environment, it messes us up mentally and emotionally, preventing us from thriving and fully contributing to our teams. Addressing this misalignment is crucial for fostering a workplace where everyone can belong and feel valued.

The trauma of misalignment in the workplace is not just an emotional burden; it poses significant dangers to our health and well-being. Constantly navigating an environment where our values and needs are disregarded leads to chronic stress, which can manifest in various physical and mental health issues. This prolonged state of tension can result in anxiety, depression, and burnout. The body's stress response, when activated over long periods, can weaken the immune system, increase blood pressure, and contribute to heart disease. And more! Consistently high cortisol levels also lead to metabolic issues/dysfunction, sleep disturbances, and psychiatric disorders. Moreover, the psychological impact of feeling disconnected and undervalued erodes our self-esteem and sense of identity, making it difficult to form meaningful relationships both inside and outside of work.

Trauma is trauma. A lot of the time people feel bad talking about workplace trauma—as if it is less traumatic than other traumas. I'm here to tell you, it's not less than, trauma is trauma.

No matter where it comes from, work-based trauma is just as impactful as any other type. Like any other trauma, work-based trauma deserves to be recognized and addressed with compassion and seriousness. We need to create supportive, inclusive workplaces where everyone feels valued and understood, ensuring that we protect and nurture our holistic health and well-being. When we experience trauma in the workplace, whether through misalignment of values, persistent stress, or feeling undervalued, it leaves deep psychological scars. The impact of work-based trauma can mirror other personal traumas, leading to anxiety, depression, and long-term health issues. The constant strain of trying to fit into an environment that doesn't meet us where we are can erode our mental health, disrupt our sense of identity, and diminish our overall well-being. It fucks up our belonging and us—it's trauma—but we have to keep going, for our livelihood and all. Plus, we're not quitters. But should we be?

Headed into the next chapter, answer these questions:

1. **Is your health suffering from your job in any way?**

_____

2. **On Sunday night, do you dread work the next morning or are you excited to get to it?**

_____

3. **Do you dread when your manager schedules a one-on-one meeting with you?**

_____

4. **If you could afford it, would you quit tomorrow?**

_____

5. **Do you feel like giving up the fight?**

_____

Did you answer yes to any of the questions? If so, keep reading.

Chapter 7

The Path Forward

Before we get to the path forward, my editor is telling me I need to recap with you all since it's been a minute. I feel like we've been through it together having explored the questions of "Who am I?" and "Where do I belong?" Asking ourselves these questions sets the stage for understanding our intrinsic need to be part of something larger without sacrificing ourselves. We then delved into the trauma-informed state of the workplace, highlighting how past experiences and workplace dynamics influence our well-being and sense of security, which led us to dive into workplace bravery. Next, we uncovered just how much we're in it together and the crucial role that leaders play at work and how they impact our lives outside of the workplace as well. Then, we dove into our values and how they align (or don't align) with our workplace. Now the time has come for us to determine the way forward.

As we conclude, "The Path Forward" serves as a roadmap for making critical decisions about staying or leaving a workplace, and if you are staying, how to brave it. This chapter will guide you in assessing your current situation and deciding the best path for your professional and personal well-being. Even though we're in it together, let's focus on you. Right about now, you are probably thinking, *do I belong here?* and *do I want to belong here?* by looking at your workplace setting and the quality of fit for you in relation to that setting. Notice I said, "quality of fit" and not "how well you fit in."

In case you didn't know, according to Bruce Banner/Hulk in *Avengers: Endgame*, you can't change the past via time travel. No, when you travel back in time, you create a new branch of reality unrelated to the one you originally came from. I find this thoroughly unsatisfying because if I went back in time, I should be able to orchestrate the outcome, *not* find myself in an equally unpredictable situation. But the truth is, with or without time travel, when we try and determine whether we should stay or go in a certain set of circumstances, there are no foolproof identifiable predictors we can look to that can ensure our future happiness. At best, we can try and unpack what is important to us in the here and now, and then scrutinize that against what we are willing to put up with.

Gauge Your Potential for Change

Gauging the potential for change involves a deep dive into our hearts and minds, acknowledging both the discomfort and the hope that comes with transformation. When we assess whether to stay in a situation or move on, it's crucial to reflect on the stories we tell ourselves about our capacity to grow and adapt. Are we clinging to old narratives out of fear, or are we open to the possibility that change can bring greater fulfillment and connection?

Are we afraid of growth because growth can feel like loss? Growth can feel like loss because, in moving forward, we often have to let go of parts of ourselves, our past, or our comfort zones. When we grow, we leave behind familiar habits, routines, and sometimes even relationships that no longer serve us. Loss surfaces because growth is a transition—an emotional journey from the known to the unknown, which can feel unsettling and lonely at times. We may grieve the simplicity or ease of what came before, or we may struggle with the uncertainty of what lies ahead. But ultimately, like loss, growth holds the potential for renewal and transformation, inviting us to embrace new possibilities and deeper layers of ourselves that can only emerge through change. We may even love the new version of ourselves.

Embrace the vulnerability that comes with uncertainty and listen to the quiet whispers of your inner self. These whispers often carry the truth about whether your current environment supports your growth or stifles it. Braving the workplace means being yourself in a world that tells you to be something different every day, and this bravery can guide you toward environments that truly nurture your sense of belonging and potential.

Belonging is a critical lens through which to view potential change. Consider whether your current setting fosters a true sense of belonging, where your presence and perspectives are genuinely appreciated. Reflect on the moments when you felt valued, seen for who you are, and connected—were they frequent or rare? Reflect on your interactions and relationships—are they nurturing and encouraging, or do they leave you feeling isolated and undervalued? Change can be daunting, but it becomes a catalyst for greater belonging. Choosing change isn't just about finding a new place; it's about finding a better place where you can thrive, where your contributions are acknowledged, and where you can be part of a community that supports and elevates you and learning how to best support yourself without sacrificing who you are.

So how do you do that? How do you use belonging as your compass for gauging your potential for change? This gauging and reflection will help you determine if your current path aligns with your need for belonging or if it's time to seek out a new horizon. This honest evaluation will guide you in making decisions that honor your needs and aspirations, paving the way for a future where you feel a true sense of belonging and connection.

Are you ready to let go? Let the gauging begin.

Assess Where You Are and Where You Want to Be

Set Your Goals

Setting a clear goal should be the first step of any decision-making process, where you define what you want to achieve. This stage involves setting clear, specific, and achievable goals. It answers the question, "What do you want to accomplish?" Your turn, high-level. What do you want to accomplish?

Questions to ask yourself:

- What do I want to achieve?

- Why is this goal important to me?

- When do I want to achieve it?

- What happens if I don't take this action? What are the consequences?

In defining your goal, make it SMART:

- **Specific:** Clearly define what you want to achieve. Avoid vague statements.

- **Measurable:** Ensure the goal has criteria for measuring progress.

- **Achievable:** Set a realistic goal that is attainable.

- **Relevant:** Ensure the goal aligns with broader objectives or personal values.

- **Time-bound:** Set a deadline for achieving the goal.

Examples of Goals:

- Decide whether to stay with or leave the company within the next six months.

- Map out my way forward to brave the workplace in my current environment over the next three months.

Your Goals:

_____

_____

_____

_____

_____

_____

Evaluate Your Reality and Obstacles

Start by conducting a thorough and honest evaluation of your current situation. This involves identifying your current job satisfaction level, understanding the specific factors contributing to any dissatisfaction, and recognizing any barriers to your goals. Gather relevant data, such as feedback from colleagues, performance reviews, and personal reflections. Assess your skills, resources, and support systems, and consider how these align with your career aspirations and values. Start high-level with questions that determine where you currently stand. After that, get more granular and particular to each goal to allow you to better identify the gap between your present state and your desired goal, which is crucial for determining the most effective steps forward.

Something to consider: "the story we tell ourselves" significantly affects our reality by shaping our perceptions, attitudes, and behaviors. This internal narrative, which consists of our beliefs, assumptions, and interpretations of experiences, influences how we see ourselves and the world around us. When the story we tell ourselves is positive and empowering, it can boost our confidence, motivation, and resilience, helping us overcome challenges and achieve our goals. Conversely, a negative or limiting narrative can create self-doubt, fear, and anxiety, leading to avoidance of risks, decreased performance, and missed opportunities. By becoming aware of and actively reshaping our internal stories, we can alter our perceptions and reactions, thereby transforming our reality and unlocking our potential for growth and success. To uncover the truth, the reality in the stories we tell ourselves, start by examining the evidence that either supports or contradicts these narratives. Reflect on your past experiences and outcomes, and seek the perspectives of trusted friends or family to gain fresh insights. This balanced approach helps to identify cognitive biases, leading to a more accurate and compassionate understanding of your personal reality.

Questions to ask yourself:

- How would I describe my current situation?

- Briefly, what has been happening?

- What have I tried so far?

- What were the results?

- What is my sense of the obstacles for me?

- What different ways might others describe the situation?

- Is my goal still realistic?

- What evidence do I have that supports or contradicts this story I'm telling myself?

- How might a trusted friend or family member view this situation differently from me?

Examples of more specific questions to ask yourself against the goal examples above to determine your reality:

- **EXAMPLE GOAL: Ask for a promotion or decide whether to stay with or leave the company within the next six months.**

  - Current Job Satisfaction:

    » How satisfied am I with my current role on a scale of one to ten?

    » What aspects of my job do I enjoy the most? What aspects do I find most frustrating or dissatisfying?

- Current Experience:

  » What has been my recent experience at work?

  » What actions have I taken so far to address my concerns or improve my situation?

- Current Sense of Belonging:

  » Do I feel a genuine sense of belonging in my current workplace?

  » Are there moments when I feel like I need to hide parts of my identity to fit in?

- Alignment with Values and Goals:

  » How well does my current job align with my long-term career goals and personal values?

  » Do I see opportunities for growth and advancement in my current role or company?

- Work Environment:

  » How would I describe the company culture? Do I feel a sense of belonging and inclusion?

  » How are my relationships with my colleagues, supervisor, and team members? Are they supportive and collaborative?

- Personal Well-Being:

  » How is my current job affecting my work-life balance and overall well-being?

  » Do I feel stressed, overwhelmed, or burned out in my current role?

  » How does my job influence my sense of belonging?

- Opportunities and Challenges:

  » What opportunities for professional development and career advancement are available to me within the company?

  » What are the main challenges and obstacles I face in my current job? Are they likely to change soon?

- Feedback and Performance:

  » What feedback have I received from my peers, supervisors, and performance reviews?

  » How do others perceive my contributions and performance?

- External Considerations:

  » Are there any external factors (e.g., family, health, personal commitments) influencing my decision to stay or leave?

- **EXAMPLE GOAL: Map out my way forward to brave the workplace in my current environment over the next three months.**

  - Current Challenges:

    » What are the specific challenges I am facing in my current role?

    » What situations or tasks do I find most difficult to handle?

  - Support Systems:

    » What support systems do I currently have in place (e.g., mentors, colleagues, resources)?

    » How can I leverage these support systems to navigate my challenges?

  - Skills and Strengths:

- » What skills and strengths do I have that can help me overcome these challenges?

- » Are there any areas where I need to develop new skills or improve existing ones?

- Actionable Steps:

  - » What specific actions can I take to address my current challenges and improve my situation?

  - » How can I break these actions into manageable steps with clear timelines?

- Feedback and Reflection:

  - » What feedback have I received regarding my performance and approach to challenges?

  - » How can I use this feedback to inform my way forward?

- Personal Well-Being:

  - » How can I ensure I maintain a healthy work-life balance while addressing these challenges?

  - » What self-care practices can I incorporate to support my well-being?

- Measuring Progress:

  - » How will I measure my progress in navigating my current work environment?

  - » What milestones or indicators will help me know I am on the right track?

Examples of Realities:

- Current job satisfaction is low due to factors like a lack of belonging, high stress levels, and limited growth opportunities.

- The decision to stay or leave will impact both personal and professional life significantly.

- Need to assess personal values, career goals, and the current work environment.

- I don't feel connected to my workplace, manager, and/ or my team.

- I can afford to quit, or I can't afford to quit due to finances.

- I don't feel a sense of belonging at work.

- I don't feel like I can be myself at work.

Your Realities:

_____

_____

_____

_____

_____

Face the Obstacles

One of the questions to ask above was, "What is my sense of the obstacles for me?" Take this a step further: To assess obstacles effectively, identify and understand both internal and external barriers that may impede your progress toward your goal. Begin by reflecting on personal challenges such as skill gaps, time constraints, or limiting beliefs that might hinder your success.

Then, consider external factors like organizational culture, resource availability, or support from colleagues and supervisors. Gathering feedback from others can provide additional insights into obstacles you may not have recognized. By analyzing these barriers from multiple perspectives, you can develop strategies to address them and create a more realistic and actionable plan for achieving your goal.

Questions to ask yourself:

- What specific challenges or barriers have I encountered while working toward this goal?

- Are these obstacles within my control, or are they influenced by external factors?

- What resources or support systems do I have that can help me overcome these obstacles?

- How have I successfully navigated similar challenges in the past, and what strategies can I apply here?

Examples of more specific questions to ask yourself against the goal examples above to face the obstacles present:

- **EXAMPLE GOAL: Decide whether to stay with or leave the company within the next six months.**
  - Internal Conflicts:
    - » What specific aspects of my job are causing me dissatisfaction or distress?
    - » Are there any personal beliefs or values that conflict with my work environment?
    - » Do I feel a genuine sense of belonging and inclusion within my current workplace, and how does this impact my decision?

» How do I live with leaving a job and risking financial setbacks?

- External Challenges:

  » What external factors (e.g., company culture, management practices) are contributing to my uncertainty about staying or leaving?

  » Are there opportunities for growth and improvement within the company that I have not yet explored?

- Support and Resources:

  » What support systems (e.g., mentors, colleagues) do I have to help me navigate this decision?

  » What additional resources or information do I need to make an informed choice?

- Past Experiences:

  » How have I dealt with similar decisions in the past, and what can I learn from those experiences?

  » What strategies or approaches have been effective for me in overcoming work-related challenges before?

- **EXAMPLE GOAL: Map out my way forward to brave the workplace in my current environment over the next three months.**

  - Current Challenges:

    » What are the main obstacles or difficulties I am facing in my current work environment?

    » Are these challenges related to specific tasks, relationships, or organizational structures? Are those likely to change soon?

  - Control and Influence:

> » Which of these obstacles are within my control to change or influence?

> » What external factors are affecting my ability to navigate the workplace, and how can I mitigate their impact?

So, what did you decide? Are you meeting your goals? Can you get a firm grasp on your reality and the obstacles that are in the way? *Are you ready for change?*

The Path Forward—Should I Stay or Should I Go?

If you are serious about changing your life you'll find a way; if not, you'll find an excuse. This isn't just about determination; it's about vulnerability and bravery. Real change requires us to step into the unknown, embrace discomfort, and face our fears head-on. It's about recognizing that the path to transformation is often riddled with obstacles and setbacks but choosing to persist anyway. When we find excuses, it's usually our way of protecting ourselves from the vulnerability that comes with stepping out of our comfort zones. But true growth happens when we allow ourselves to be seen and take that brave step forward, even when it's hard. And on this journey, finding a sense of belonging can be your anchor—reminding you that you're not alone and that you've leveled up in knowing who you are. You know your worth, you trust your potential, and you're ready to take on whatever's next.

Is It Possible for Me to Brave the Workplace in My Current Adventure or Is It Time for a New One?

Deciding whether to stay at or leave your current job is one of the boldest and most gut-level honest choices you can make. It's like peeling back layers to reveal what you truly want, facing the raw truth of your own happiness, and having the grit to choose what feels right deep down. It's about deeply listening to yourself, trusting your gut, and honoring your truth. True belonging doesn't require us to change who we are; it requires us to *be* who we are. You wrote down your goals, reality, and obstacles but you're still standing at a crossroads. Now ask yourself: *do I feel like I belong here?*

Take a moment to reflect on your daily experiences at work. Do you feel seen, heard, and valued? Or are you constantly battling a sense of invisibility and exclusion? True belonging at work means being part of something larger without sacrificing your authenticity. If your workplace encourages you to show up as your true self, fosters meaningful connections, and aligns with your core values, that's a sign you're in a place where you can thrive. But if you find yourself constantly compromising your well-being to fit in, masking your true feelings, or feeling emotionally exhausted, it's time to reconsider (remember the dangers of sacrificial belonging and the emotional toll it takes). If your job is causing you to sacrifice your health, values, or happiness, it's not serving you well.

Making this decision also involves considering your future growth. Ask yourself: *Is this job helping me grow, both personally and professionally?* Am I excited about the opportunities here, or do I feel stagnant and unfulfilled? Your work should be a place where you can continue to learn, contribute, and expand your potential. Ultimately, the decision to stay or leave is about trusting yourself and what you need to feel a true sense of belonging. It's about finding a place where you can be brave, show up fully, and know that you matter. Remember, you deserve to be in an environment that celebrates your uniqueness and supports your journey. Trust yourself, get clear on what you need, and choose the path that aligns with who you really are.

On the one hand, staying can offer a stable environment if you've built meaningful relationships and understand the organizational culture. These connections can provide a sense of security and camaraderie, fostering emotional well-being and a supportive network. When you feel truly seen and valued, your work becomes more than just a job—it transforms into a place where you can thrive, contribute, and grow. This sense of belonging can drive motivation, creativity, and a willingness to go above and beyond, knowing that your efforts are appreciated and your voice matter. On the other hand, don't let your loyalty keep you in a place that common sense should get you out of.

Speaking of common sense, let's outline significant reasons to seriously consider leaving that require careful thought and consideration:

- **Your sense of belonging feels thwarted or sacrificial**. If you're sacrificing your well-being to fit in or pretending to align with the culture, you're not genuinely connected. If you find yourself constantly masking your true self, feeling invisible, or feeling excluded, it's a clear sign that your current environment isn't supporting you. You deserve a place where you can show up fully and be valued for who you are by others and where you have pride in yourself.

- **Your workplace is compromising your mental and physical health**. Then it's time to consider leaving. Chronic stress, adjustment disorders (see below), anxiety, and unhealthy burnout are powerful signals that your environment is toxic. Your well-being should never be sacrificed for a job. Workplace trauma and stress can have a profound impact on your physical health, manifesting in various ways beyond chronic stress, anxiety, and burnout. A toxic work environment can lead to cardiovascular problems such as high blood pressure and heart disease, gastrointestinal issues like irritable bowel syndrome and stomach ulcers, and a weakened immune system, making you more susceptible to infections. Musculoskeletal pain, including tension headaches, migraines, neck pain, and lower back pain, is also common, as is the disruption of sleep patterns, leading to insomnia or chronic fatigue. Additionally, stress can cause significant weight fluctuations due to changes in appetite, eating habits, and metabolic dysfunction resulting from high cortisol levels. These physical symptoms are your body's way of signaling that something is wrong. Remember, you are worthy of a space that nurtures your health, not depletes it.

- **You are sacrificing or diminishing your integrity, personal values, and morals**. If your workplace consistently forces you to act against your principles or ethical standards, the dissonance can erode your sense of self and cause immense internal conflict. Upholding your values is crucial for maintaining your self-respect and inner peace.

- **You are experiencing stagnant growth and a lack of opportunities for advancement, and it is stifling your potential**. If you're not learning, growing, or being challenged in meaningful ways, you're not reaching your full potential. Environments that don't foster growth lead

to disengagement and dissatisfaction. You deserve a
workplace that invests in your development and recognizes
your contributions.

- **You need to reclaim your life outside of work**. If your job
  consumes all your time and energy, leaving you with little
  room for personal fulfillment, relationships, or hobbies, it's
  worth reevaluating. Balance is essential for a fulfilling life,
  and no job should dominate your existence.

Here are some serious conditions (primarily stress-induced)
that we don't speak about often enough impacting our sense of
belonging and physical health referenced above.

Work-Induced Adjustment Disorder

Adjustment disorder is a tough and often misunderstood
condition. It's when the stress of life's changes or challenges
becomes too overwhelming, and our usual coping mechanisms
can't keep up. Imagine you're trying to navigate a stormy sea
without a life jacket—every wave feels like it could pull you
under. That's what it feels like when our ability to adapt gets
overloaded. When you're dealing with adjustment disorder, even
small tasks can feel insurmountable because your mind and
heart are constantly wrestling with a sense of imbalance and
unease. It's marked by feelings of anxiety, sadness, and difficulty
concentrating. It's a reminder that sometimes, we need extra
support and compassion to weather life's storms.

With that said, allow me to introduce you to **Work-induced
adjustment order**. Work-induced adjustment disorder happens
when the stress and demands of our job become too much for
us to handle, and our usual ways of coping don't cut it. When

there is a lack of values alignment between an employee and their organization, it can also create a chronic state of stress and internal conflict leading to work-induced adjustment disorder. It's like trying to hold it all together with a smile on your face while feeling like you're falling apart inside. The constant pressure and misalignment with our work environment can lead to intense feelings of unease, sadness, stress, internal conflict, and even hopelessness. Employees may experience symptoms like anxiety, depression, and difficulty concentrating. It's not just about having a bad day at work; it's a persistent struggle that affects our ability to function both professionally and personally. When we're forced to navigate a workplace that doesn't align with our values or support our well-being, it can take a serious toll on our mental health, leaving us feeling isolated and overwhelmed.

Workplace-induced adjustment disorder is a distinct form of adjustment disorder that emerges within the work environment. Unlike broader adjustment challenges, individuals with this disorder may adapt well to changes in other areas of life yet struggle intensely in their workplace. This disorder arises from ongoing tension between personal values and the demands or culture of a misaligned work setting. As employees try to balance their true selves with the expectations placed on them, a powerful cognitive dissonance develops, gradually eroding their mental health.

Affected employees often withdraw from social interactions, avoid collaboration, and find it difficult to maintain professional relationships, further isolating them. Forced to conform in ways that feel misaligned with their identity, they enter a cycle of emotional strain, exacerbating disengagement and loneliness. Workplace-induced adjustment disorder can manifest as heightened anxiety, constant worry, and even dread about work, making everyday tasks feel overwhelming. Impacted individuals may experience a profound sense of helplessness, cynicism, or loss of motivation, and some may adopt "sacrificial" belonging, sacrificing personal values to fit in or "try to belong." Together, these symptoms reveal a significant struggle to cope with workplace demands.

Workplace-Related Avoidance Disorder

Avoidance disorder, more commonly referred to as Avoidant Personality Disorder (AvPD), is a condition characterized by feelings of inadequacy and sensitivity to rejection. People with this disorder often go to great lengths to avoid social interactions and situations where they might be judged, criticized, or rejected. They may crave close relationships but fear them intensely, leading to a pattern of social withdrawal and isolation. This disorder is marked by a persistent avoidance of activities that involve significant interpersonal contact due to fears of criticism, disapproval, or rejection. It's not just about being shy or introverted; it's a pervasive and chronic condition that significantly impacts an individual's ability to lead a fulfilling life. How does this relate to the workplace?

Workplace-Related Avoidance Disorder happens when employees feel so overwhelmed by fear of criticism, rejection, or failure that they start to withdraw from work-related activities and interactions. It's like having a constant, nagging voice in your head telling you that you're not good enough, that you don't belong, and that any mistake will expose you as a fraud, or anything "less than." This fear can lead to avoiding team meetings, shying away from projects that require collaboration, and even avoiding casual conversations with colleagues. It's not just about being introverted or needing some alone time (extroverts and ambiverts experience this too); it's a deep-seated anxiety that makes every interaction feel like a potential threat.

Let's take Lorelai, for example. She is a high achiever and has difficulty communicating with her manager—she calls her the dinosaur (we'll call her Dino). Dino is a typical old-school female manager raised as a leader in a world of men that she tried to emulate and so she plays down being a woman in a male-dominated industry. Dino is a polarizing figure, loudly favoring certain employees while dismissing or undermining others, creating division and resentment within the team. Lorelai cancels her one-on-one meetings telling Dino it is to give her time back. She overachieves to avoid her, and she is rewarded for it. Dino loves when Lorelai gives her time back to get other things done, so Dino then praises Lorelai and in turn, Lorelai's moods lift—until the next one-on-one looms and Lorelai's stomach is tied in knots the day before.

Let's break this down. Lorelai's behavior of avoiding Dino and canceling one-on-one meetings may stem from a combination of factors. Firstly, Dino being a polarizing figure likely creates discomfort or tension in their interactions, making it challenging to communicate openly. This discomfort may lead Lorelai to seek ways to minimize direct contact with Dino to avoid potential conflict or negative interactions. Additionally, Lorelai's perception of Dino may further reinforce her avoidance behavior, as she may believe Dino does not have time for her concerns or feedback. Lorelai's tendency to avoid Dino could be a coping mechanism to compensate for the perceived lack of support or guidance from Dino and give her a sense of control and validation independent of her interactions with Dino. When Lorelai is being rewarded for overachievement, it reinforces the belief that avoiding direct communication with Dino is a successful strategy for achieving goals and receiving recognition in the workplace. However, it's essential to recognize that long-term avoidance can hinder effective communication and collaboration, ultimately impacting professional and personal growth.

People are often rewarded in the workplace for avoidance behaviors due to various factors within the organizational culture and leadership dynamics. One reason could be a focus on short-term results or immediate problem-solving, where avoiding difficult conversations or conflicts may appear to offer a quick resolution without addressing underlying issues. Additionally, organizational structures or incentives may inadvertently reinforce avoidance by prioritizing efficiency over effective communication or conflict resolution. Sometimes, people turn to avoidance as a quick fix to dodge discomfort or sidestep potential backlash. Sure, it might feel like a relief at the moment, but in the long run, it can make things worse. In some workplaces, leaders unknowingly reinforce this pattern by not offering enough support or guidance in handling tough situations, unintentionally sending the message that avoiding issues is an okay way to cope.

When workplace-related avoidance sets in, it severely impacts our sense of belonging. Belonging is all about feeling connected, valued, and accepted for who we are—not just by our peers, managers, and companies but also by ourselves. But when we start to avoid interactions out of fear of judgment or rejection, we cut ourselves off from the connections that foster true belonging. Without those meaningful connections and authentic interactions, we start to feel invisible and undervalued. We miss out on the collaborative spirit that makes work fulfilling and the camaraderie that helps us through challenging times. Instead of participating in team activities, coaching sessions with managers, sharing our ideas, or seeking support from colleagues, we retreat into isolation. This withdrawal not only heightens our feelings of inadequacy but also creates a vicious cycle where the lack of interaction and engagement further deepens our sense of disconnection. Over time, avoidance can erode our self-esteem and sense of belonging, making it even harder to break the cycle. Over time, this eroded sense of belonging can lead to decreased job satisfaction, lower motivation, and even mental health issues like anxiety and depression. It's a stark reminder that belonging isn't just about being physically present; it's about feeling genuinely connected and valued in our workplace community. Overall, addressing avoidance behavior in the workplace requires a shift toward fostering true belonging, open communication, psychological safety, and a culture that values proactive problem-solving and constructive conflict resolution.

Burnout

Burnout, as defined by Dr. Kandi Wiens, is a psychological syndrome that arises from prolonged exposure to work-related stress.[31] It is not just feeling tired after a long week; it's a deep, pervasive state of physical, emotional, and mental exhaustion caused by prolonged and excessive stress at work. Imagine the relentless pressure of always needing to be "on" while feeling like you're constantly falling short. It's the emotional drain from giving too much of yourself without feeling like you're making a meaningful impact. It's when your enthusiasm and motivation have been ground down by the demands of your job, leaving you feeling cynical, detached, and ineffective. Burnout is characterized by emotional exhaustion, depersonalization, and a reduced sense of personal accomplishment. When employees experience burnout, they feel drained, cynical, and ineffective, which deeply impacts their professional and personal lives. In the workplace, burnout manifests in various ways, including decreased productivity, increased absenteeism, and a lack of engagement. Employees might struggle to concentrate, feel disconnected from their colleagues, and lose the motivation that once drove their work. Again, burnout is more than feeling tired; it's a state of chronic stress that can lead to serious mental and physical health issues if not addressed.

When there's misalignment between employees and their workplace, the persistent effort required to hide their true selves and values leads to burnout as they sacrifice their well-being to maintain an illusion of alignment. We might find ourselves compromising our principles or engaging in work that feels meaningless or ethically uncomfortable, leading to increased stress and dissatisfaction. This constant dissonance requires a great deal of emotional energy to navigate, which can quickly deplete our mental and emotional reserve, leading to serious consequences.

If You Do Decide to Leave

Is quitting right for you right now? Leaving your workplace is a profound decision, and it's crucial to weigh the significant drawbacks, especially those related to your health. For me, I know it's on my mind a lot when my quitting song ("Shout" by Tears for Fears) pops into my head.[32] Many of us have an anthem that makes us feel something like quitting or empowerment to quit. Makes sense since music enhances our sense of belonging to self. What's yours? How often are you playing it (out loud or in your head)? While jamming, there are some critical considerations that we often overlook in our quest for belonging, so let's dig in.

First, let's talk about the stress and anxiety that can accompany the uncertainty of leaving a job. Your workplace might not be perfect, but it's a known quantity. Stepping into the unknown can spike your stress levels, impacting your mental health and overall well-being. In addition, it's stressful when we think of what quitting impacts. For me, I stress thinking that quitting means something less for my family—less money, less opportunity, less in general. The idea of not giving them what they need breaks me even though the job itself is breaking me and most likely I cannot be my best or give them my best because of the stress of it all. You might find yourself losing sleep, feeling anxious, or even experiencing physical symptoms like headaches or stomach issues. It's your body's way of telling you that change, while sometimes necessary, isn't easy. Next, there's the risk of losing your support network. Even in challenging environments, we often have colleagues who offer friendship and support. Leaving means stepping away from these relationships, which can leave you feeling isolated and disconnected. These social bonds are vital for your mental and emotional health, providing a buffer against the stresses of work. Additionally, consider the financial instability that might come with leaving. Even with a solid plan, there's always a period of adjustment that can strain your finances. This financial stress can exacerbate feelings of insecurity and anxiety, further affecting your mental health. Finally, let's not forget the impact on your sense of identity and purpose. Work gives us a structure and a sense of purpose. Losing that can leave a void, leading to feelings of loss and uncertainty about your future. It's essential to recognize that your job often forms a part of your identity and leaving it can trigger an identity challenge.

Also, even when you leave your job, if you don't process the factors that caused you to leave, they may follow you via Workplace PTSD. Unresolved trauma can manifest in new environments, affecting your emotional and physical well-being. Symptoms like hypervigilance, avoidance, and flashbacks can persist, impacting your ability to trust new colleagues and fully engage in your work. It's crucial to address the root causes of your distress through therapy, self-reflection, and supportive networks. For example, many survivors of toxic jobs wrestle with a crushing worry that they might have been able to stop the abuse if they had acted differently, and that stays with them even when they leave the manager, the job, the team, the company. Those with high emotional intelligence are particularly self-reflective. They start to question themselves: *How could I have done things differently? How could I have prevented this?* This self-reflection can spiral into rumination, a nonstop loop of thoughts that don't lead to change but instead continually release stress hormones. Replaying the abuse in their minds, trying to figure out what they could have done differently, only deepens their pain and suffering and ultimately erodes their sense of belonging. Over time, this can wreak havoc on our minds and wear down our bodies, causing or exacerbating stress-related illnesses like diabetes, high blood pressure, and cardiac issues. Healing from workplace trauma is a process, and by confronting these issues head-on, you can break free from the cycle of trauma and build a healthier, more fulfilling professional life and clear the path to thrive in a new job. We feel the painful sensations and try to run from them because it's easier than feeling them. But that's the funny thing about trauma and grief: feelings of loss, even for a job we're choosing to leave, wait for us—so, deal with the trauma now or the trauma will deal with you later.

Leaving a job isn't always an easy decision, but trusting yourself and prioritizing your health, values, and growth is a powerful act of self-respect. Crank up your anthem (or even your quitting playlist if you have one), take a deep breath, reflect on your inner strength, and empower yourself to do what will serve you best. Ask yourself, do you have the resilience to drive positive change in your current environment, or is it wearing down your sense of self? Your decision should honor your capacity to thrive and uphold your sense of belonging. Choose the path that nurtures your authentic self and allows you to grow. Lean into your support network—talk to mentors, trusted colleagues, and career coaches. Their insights can illuminate your path, helping you see possibilities and pitfalls you might have missed. Remember, you don't have to navigate this alone; external perspectives are vital in making an informed decision. You are worthy of a workplace that honors and nurtures all that you are.

If You Decide to Stay

Choose yourself instead of choosing to endure. This means setting boundaries that protect your well-being and advocating for your needs unapologetically. Start by identifying what truly matters to you—the way you experience belonging, your values, passions, and nonnegotiables. Communicate these clearly to your team and leadership, and don't be afraid to say no when tasks or expectations threaten your balance. Invest in self-care rituals that replenish your energy and keep you grounded. Seek out mentors and allies who uplift and support you, creating a network of encouragement. Practice vulnerability by sharing your struggles and aspirations, fostering authentic connections and a sense of belonging. Remember, staying doesn't mean sacrificing your happiness; it means cultivating an environment where you can thrive. You deserve to feel valued, fulfilled, and truly part of the team, not just present. By choosing yourself and your sense of belonging, you honor your worth and pave the way for a more meaningful and empowered work experience.

Another thing—just like you had a quitting anthem, have one for staying. For me, since I am a little passionate, always coming in hot, my staying song is "Seven Nation Army" by the White Stripes.[33] I kind of liken mine to feeling like it's my closing song (like pitchers have in baseball) and the song gives me a ton of energy. My friend Lisa's staying song is "The Bones" by Maren Morris; it is calmer, and the words put her at ease.[34] What's your staying anthem?

Set Boundaries

What does it mean to set boundaries? Establishing limits and defining what is acceptable or unacceptable to you in various aspects of your life, such as relationships, work, personal space, and emotional well-being. How can you set boundaries in the workplace specifically? Same approach: defining what is acceptable and unacceptable behavior, communication, workload, and expectations within the work environment and establishing limits and guidelines regarding your professional life.

The important takeaway here: this is about *you*. When most people talk about setting boundaries, they miss something crucial—you can't control other people. Boundary setting should not be your way of telling other people what they can and cannot do. Boundaries help you maintain your autonomy, protect your values, and ensure that your needs and preferences are respected. Setting workplace boundaries involves clearly communicating your limits, expectations, and personal boundaries to others. It requires understanding your needs and recognizing when those needs are being compromised or violated. By setting boundaries, you are drawing a line between what is acceptable behavior and what is not, which helps foster healthier relationships and self-care. In the quest for true belonging, it's essential to know what you need and what you won't sacrifice, ensuring that your sense of self remains intact. For example, here are some of the boundaries that I've set in the workplace for myself.

- **Workload and time management:** I set boundaries regarding my workload around how much I can handle and by communicating to my manager, my peers, and my team's colleagues or superiors around realistic deadlines, avoiding taking on excessive tasks, and my work hours. I eat lunch at my desk, take a break to pick up my kids from 1:00–1:30 p.m. and won't take meetings during that time. I spend time cooking and eating dinner from 5:00–7:00 p.m. I may go back online to work at night but that doesn't mean I will take meetings at night and I don't expect it of others.

- **Communication:** I set boundaries in how I want to be contacted and when I prefer to be contacted. This seems to be the trickiest for me. I set expectations for response times and appropriate channels of communication. For example, I use Slack for work from 8:00–5:00 p.m., and if it's an emergency, an after-hours text message is fine. I let people know I won't be checking Slack after around 5:00 p.m. and they should not text me from dinnertime on unless it is an emergency. Practicing what you preach helps here. I also ask others how they communicate best—it helps us all manage interruptions and minimize distractions.

- **Role and responsibilities:** I set boundaries by clearly defining my role and responsibilities with my manager, peers, and team to help set what I am accountable for and what falls outside of my scope of work. You may be thinking, *that won't fly in my organization—my manager tells me what I do.* Just try it, I dare you. If worse comes to worst, it's a discussion or negotiation with your manager. For me, it helps prevent me from being overwhelmed by tasks that do not align with my role or expertise. It also reduces frustration from being assigned tasks outside of my function. The key here is to communicate and clarify your boundaries with your manager first, then go on your press tour.

- **My assertiveness:** I set boundaries by saying no when necessary. It usually means respectfully declining tasks or requests beyond my capacity or not aligned with my goals and priorities. It helps avoid overcommitment and ensures that my time and energy are focused on the most important tasks. Some people fit into the camp of saying yes to everything, which leads to overwork and burnout. While you don't want to become a no person, align to your focus—if it's out of scope, put it out of mind.

Boundaries can be physical, emotional, or even mental. For example, physical boundaries involve defining your personal space and determining who can touch you or enter your personal space. Emotional boundaries pertain to expressing your emotions and establishing limits on what kind of emotional support you are willing to provide or receive. Mental boundaries relate to protecting your thoughts, beliefs, and opinions, and setting limits on what information or influences you allow into your life.

It is important to remember that setting boundaries is not about being selfish or rigid; it is about self-respect, self-care, and maintaining healthy relationships. When you set clear boundaries, you create a framework that allows you to prioritize your well-being while also fostering mutual respect and understanding with others.

My Final Wish for You

Remember, braving the workplace means being yourself in a world that tells you to be something different every day. Being brave in the workplace when your values don't align with those of the organization means having the courage to stand up for what you believe in, even when it's difficult. It starts with knowing yourself deeply—principles, flaws, and all. Engage in open and honest conversations with your leaders and colleagues about your concerns. Frame these discussions around the benefits that aligning workplace practices with your values can bring to the team and organization, such as increased trust, collaboration, and long-term success. Focus on celebrating your wins. How do you cheer yourself on?

Additionally, bravery involves setting clear boundaries to protect your well-being. This might mean saying no to tasks that compromise your principles or seeking out projects that align more closely with your values. Surround yourself with a support network of colleagues who understand and respect your stance, providing a buffer against feeling isolated. Practicing self-care is also essential to maintain your resilience and strength. Remember, it's about making decisions that honor your core beliefs, advocating for positive change where possible, and knowing when it's time to move on if the misalignment becomes too detrimental to your well-being. In essence, bravery in this context is about staying true to who you are and what you stand for, even when the road is tough.

Don't dwell on the places where you don't belong. Instead, focus on where you do belong, where your strengths are celebrated and your true self is welcomed. When you shift your perspective to seek out spaces and communities that embrace you, you open yourself up to connections and opportunities. Know your worth. Affirm your worth—don't negotiate your worth with anyone. Trust that there are environments and people out there who will appreciate you for who you are. You know who you are—you don't need anyone to tell you—especially those you would never take advice from, let alone criticism. By looking for belonging within yourself, you create a mindset that attracts positivity and acceptance, fostering deeper, more meaningful relationships. Choose to see the world as a place full of sincere, meaningful connections waiting to be made, rather than obstacles to overcome. This shift not only enhances your sense of true belonging but also empowers you to build a life filled with genuine connection and joy...bravely.

In Appreciation

"To the world you may be one person; but to one person
you may be the world."
—Dr. Seuss

When I say we are in this together—no statement could be truer.
There are *many* people that inspired, debated, encouraged, and
supported me to write this book, helping me along the way. "How
do you thank someone for taking you from crayons to perfume?
It isn't easy but I'll try" (Lulu with the Mindbenders). You all know
that my brain is 80 percent music lyrics, no surprise here.

Thank you to Scott, Drew, and the entire crew at Gray & Miller
Agency. Yaddyra, Hugo, Elina, and MJ at Mango—you all took a
chance on me and I am grateful.

Thank you to the Graduate School of Education at the University
of Pennsylvania and PennCLO for making me feel good about
being a scrappy little fighter. I used to see the bumps in the road
as uphill battles but you helped me appreciate how they make
me stronger and how to embrace my rebellious nature. Shout out
to #Multipliers. Huge thank you to Dr. Grant Gatschet—the best
memes in the game, best musical IQ, and biggest heart. Dr. Mark
Kestner, Phillip Ellis, Bonita Thompson, Lilian Ajayi-Ore, Heather
Marshall, Jen Turgeon, Antoinette Nottingham, and Jennifer Bailey
Jackson—you are inspiration goals.

Christy—I have so much love for you, beyond measure. Your smile
can light up an entire town and your care is second to none. I
am grateful for your trust in me, your insights, instincts, and
friendship, always.

Pat—I only wish we met even sooner. You make every day better than the last. We laugh so much and drive each other to be our best. Actually, you are the best and I just get to be in your glow. Your Christmas themes are the envy of us all along with your green thumb. Tricia would agree and of course, she is our favorite equestrian and a wonderful friend. Thank you, well, for everything!

As you like to say, nobody ever died from an overdose of appreciation—so here goes, Billy. I'm privileged to say I've learned from you for over fifteen years and I have no idea how I would have managed without your creative brilliance, mentorship, sense of humor, partnership, and of course, for NormaJean (the best). No one is a better leadership guru but most important, no one is a better friend than you.

V—manager turned cherished friend by which I measure all leaders by, for all of the goodness that is you. I don't know I got so lucky that you SSL took me under your wings. No other leader has taught me more than you and I am grateful. #Loveyoulongtime.

My family, with love. Heather, who always reminds me of who I am in the moments when I can't catch my breath and loves me like only a sister can. Thank you for bringing Scott into our lives. Elizabeth and Ted, Stella and Patrick, Adi and Adam. Mary and George for raising the best man that I know. Much love to the nieces and nephews I hold dear: Addison, Aidan, Grace, Jack, Bodhi, Ari, Thalia, William, Franny, Maggie, Xavier, and Estella. To Roza and Stuart Glodowski, gone but never forgotten. I think about you all of the time and hope that I've made you proud.

My friends that are chosen family: Sarah, Jaimee and Jon, Mindy and Rick, Staci and Ed, Lori and Bill, Michele and Josh, Stacy and Josh, Michelle and Craig, and all of the wonderful women at Garage Barre—love you all.

My fourth-grade teacher at Valley Elementary in Bensalem, Pennsylvania, Ms. Welch—thank you for being one of the first in my life to encourage me to use my voice. You cared about what I had to say and that meant the world. I hung on every word of your adventures about Japan and your sense of risk-taking has inspired a lot of who I am.

Paula Stone Williams—I can't believe how lucky I am to be guided by the kindest soul with the most eloquent words, best intuition, and smarts for days. I'm grateful to spend time with you and thank you for everything.

Shannon Brady for welcoming me into the belonging researcher community and being an inspiration at every turn.

Chelsea and Michelle for your editing and perspectives way before this book made it to the publisher.

To the loves of my life—Steve, Joshua, Owen, and Kelce. XOXO. LYHYKYMY. You are my everything. Follow @flyeaglesfly6666. I love you with all of my heart. More than the world love. "If the sun refused to shine, I would still be loving you. If mountains crumbled to the sea, it would still be you and me" (Led Zeppelin). A lot.

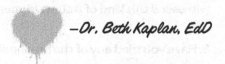

—Dr. Beth Kaplan, EdD

Book Club Questions

1. Dr. Kaplan describes belonging as the innate desire to be part of something larger than ourselves without sacrificing who we are. In what ways did the definition of belonging challenge or affirm your pre-existing beliefs about belonging?

2. When you think about your history with belonging, what memories or experiences come to mind? How about fitting in? What were the differences that stand out the most?

3. *Braving the Workplace* lists various types of belonging (true, thwarted, sacrificial, and dissimulated). Which type resonated most with you, and why? Can you relate any of these concepts to your experiences in the workplace?

4. Is work-life balance a thing? What are your experiences?

5. *Braving the Workplace* explores the journey from workplace trauma to belonging. How does workplace trauma differ from general stress or challenges at work? Have you ever experienced or witnessed this kind of trauma in your workplace?

6. Have you tried any of the healing strategies from *Braving the Workplace*? Which resonates with you the most?

7. The concept of "braving" is central to *Braving the Workplace*. How do you see this type of bravery playing out in your professional and personal lives?

8. There is an ongoing critique that traditional workplace cultures prioritize performance over well-being. What could your workplace do to strike a better balance?

9. What belonging moments and activities do you partake in when you are feeling lost? How do they make you feel more like yourself?

10. Is creating a sense of belonging at work the responsibility of the organization, the individual, or both? Do you feel the same about well-being? How do you suggest individuals take ownership of their belonging, and what steps can you personally take to enhance your sense of belonging in your work environment?

11. If you could ask Dr. Kaplan one question after reading this book, what would it be, and why? You can! Join the conversation on LinkedIn: https://www.linkedin.com/company/belonging-at-work and visit drbethkaplan.com.

About the Author

Researcher and storyteller Dr. Beth Kaplan is fascinated by the concept of belonging and how it impacts our work lives—spilling over into our personal lives. She is a renowned author and speaker specializing in the study of belonging. Beth is interested in how workplace dynamics impact our well-being and how to help the unseen, unheard, and happy feel less alone.

As a workplace executive with an EdD in learning and leadership strategy from the University of Pennsylvania, she researched belonging and workplace trauma; Beth helps companies improve their retention and culture. She is a sought-after consultant and advisor for Fortune 500 companies, nonprofits, and educational institutions. Beth loves to connect and empower audiences around the world through her writing, speaking engagements, and workshops.

Beth's research on belonging has revolutionized how leaders approach team-building and organizational culture. She is passionate about helping individuals and organizations create environments where everyone can thrive, bringing her expertise and warmth to everything she does.

Beth lives with her husband and their two boys outside of Philadelphia.

For more information about Dr. Beth Kaplan and her work, visit drbethkaplan.com.

Endnotes

1   Brené Brown, *Braving the Wilderness: The Quest for True Belonging and the Courage to Stand Alone.*

2   Brené Brown, *Dare to Lead: Brave Work. Tough Conversations. Whole Hearts.*

3   Mary Ainsworth, "The Strange Situation Technique" experiment.

4   Thomas Joiner, "The Interpersonal Theory of Suicide." *Psychological Review,* 2010 (pp. 575-600).

5   Brené Brown, *Braving the Wilderness: The Quest for True Belonging and the Courage to Stand Alone.*

6   Roy Baumeister and Mark Leary, "The Need to Belong: Desire for Interpersonal Attachments as a Fundamental Human Motivation." *Psychological Bulletin,* 1995 (pp. 497–529).

7   Thomas Joiner, "The Interpersonal Theory of Suicide." *Psychological Review,* 2010 (pp. 575-600).

8   J.K. Rowling, *Harry Potter and the Half-Blood Prince.*

9   Erving Goffman, *Stigma: Notes on the Management of Spoiled Identity.*

10 Gregory Walton and Geoffrey Cohen, *The Science of Belonging and Connection.*

11 Frank Baum, *The Wonderful Wizard of Oz.*

12 Henry Ford, *I Invented the Modern Age: The Rise of Henry Ford.*

13 Marshall Sahlins, *Stone Age Economics.*

14 Nancy Bilyeau, "Do You Work Longer Hours Than a Medieval Peasant?" Medium, 2021.

15 J.R.R. Tolkien, *The Lord of the Rings* series.

16 Jonathan Cott, *Bob Dylan: The Essential Interviews.*

17 Mike Judge, *Office Space.* Judgmental Films, 1999.

18 Leo Tolstoy, *Anna Karenina.*

19 Joss Whedon, *Buffy the Vampire Slayer.* Mutant Enemy Productions, 1997–2003.

20 Stanley Schachter, *The Psychology of Affiliation: Experimental Studies of the Sources of Gregariousness.*

21 Henri Tajfel and John Turner, "An Integrative Theory of Intergroup Conflict." *Intergroup Relations: Essential Readings,* 2001 (pp. 94–109).

22 Charles Dickens, *Oliver Twist*.

23 Jean Kantambu Latting and V. Jean Ramsey, *Reframing Change: How to Deal with Workplace Dynamics, Influence Others, and Bring People Together to Initiate Positive Change*.

24 Greg Daniels, *The Office* (US). Deedle-Dee Productions, 2005–2013. Adapted from *The Office* (UK) by Ricky Gervais.

25 American Institute of Stress, www.stress.org.

26 International Labor Organization, "Working Time and Work-Life Balance Around the World." 2022.

27 J.K. Rowling, *Harry Potter and the Philosopher's Stone*.

28 Gregory Walton and Shannon Brady, "The Social-Belonging Intervention." *Handbook of Wise Interventions: How Social Psychology Can Help People Change*, 2021 (pp. 36–62).

29 Susan Cain, *Quiet: The Power of Introverts in a World That Can't Stop Talking*.

30 Taylor Swift, "Shake It Off." *1898*, 2014.

31 Kandi Wiens, *Burnout Immunity: How Emotional Intelligence Can Help You Build Resilience and Heal Your Relationship with Work*.

32 Tears for Fears, "Shout." *Songs from the Big Chair*, 1985.

33 The White Stripes, "Seven Nation Army." *Elephant*, 2003.

34 Maren Morris, "The Bones." *Girl*, 2019.

Index

Mango Publishing, established in 2014, publishes an eclectic list of books by diverse authors—both new and established voices—on topics ranging from business, personal growth, women's empowerment, LGBTQ studies, health, and spirituality to history, popular culture, time management, decluttering, lifestyle, mental wellness, aging, and sustainable living. We were named 2019 *and* 2020's #1 fastest growing independent publisher by *Publishers Weekly*. Our success is driven by our main goal, which is to publish high-quality books that will entertain readers as well as make a positive difference in their lives.

Our readers are our most important resource; we value your input, suggestions, and ideas. We'd love to hear from you—after all, we are publishing books for you!

Please stay in touch with us and follow us at:

Facebook: Mango Publishing
Twitter: @MangoPublishing
Instagram: @MangoPublishing
LinkedIn: Mango Publishing
Pinterest: Mango Publishing
Newsletter: mangopublishinggroup.com/newsletter

Join us on Mango's journey to reinvent publishing, one book at a time.

www.ingramcontent.com/pod-product-compliance
Lightning Source LLC
Jackson TN
JSHW031102161224
74479JS00003B/5